Total Acceptance

by J. William Erickson

DORRANCE
PUBLISHING CO
EST. 1920
PITTSBURGH, PENNSYLVANIA 15238

The contents of this work, including, but not limited to, the accuracy of events, people, and places depicted; opinions expressed; permission to use previously published materials included; and any advice given or actions advocated are solely the responsibility of the author, who assumes all liability for said work and indemnifies the publisher against any claims stemming from publication of the work.

Dorrance Publishing Co
585 Alpha Drive
Suite 103
Pittsburgh, PA 15238
Visit our website at www.dorrancebookstore.com

ISBN: 978-1-4809-5463-2
eISBN: 978-1-4809-5438-0

All Bible verse quotations
from
New Scofield Study Bible
NIV Version 1984
Oxford University Press

Other Bible verse quotations
Billy Graham New Testament
Knowing Jesus Personally
Published by Billy Graham Evangelistic Assn.

This book is dedicated to
Jesus Christ; My God, My King,
My Savior, My Friend;
My Everything!

Chapter One

The Second World War had just ended, and America's fighting men and women were coming home. A man and his wife now looked for a home to buy so they could raise a family.

Portland, Oregon, was a large city straddling the Willamette River, hence the nickname of Bridgetown. Portland was basically flat on the east side of the river; the west side, however, was crowned with forested hills and more dramatic geography as you continued west. About forty miles and the Coast Range Mountains were the last barrier to the Pacific Ocean, only ten miles from Portland.

Many people who visited Portland called it God's country because of all the green. A mixture of fir, spruce, pine, alder, and various other species thrived in the rainy Oregon weather.

Only seventy miles east were the Cascade Mountains: St. Helens, Mt. Hood, and, of course, the must-see Columbia Gorge that held the Columbia River in check as it snaked its way to the Pacific.

The license plates said Pacific Wonderland, an outdoors person's dream come true. Fishing, hiking, skiing, boating, and exploring were just a few reasons people heard and had to come see it for themselves!

A boy was born to this young, married couple in the middle of winter in 1949. Their home was built in a community of new homes built for the returning veterans. The home had a big lot, room for a yard, and even an area for a garden.

The father of the boy was a hard worker and landscaped the whole back yard in stages. The garden was planted, and soon a daughter was born also.

So the scene was set: a family of four in a paradise of God's creation all around them.

An early recollection of mine was a two-week vacation Bible school in second or third grade. It is hard to remember that far back now.

> *Proverbs 22:6 "Train a child in the way that he should go and when he is old he will not turn from it."*

The family was not a regular church-on-Sunday family; rather, it was rest and recreation on weekends. But a seed had been planted in the boy, and it started to grow. Little did he realize that an enemy was plotting to sidetrack him; for over forty years, he would struggle and fail, imprisoned by this enemy who fought his escape at every turn.

The children were now going to a babysitter every day because both parents worked, and it was only the early fifties. Both parents did have good jobs and worked hard to provide for their children and themselves.

> *Ecclesiastes 3:9-13 "What does the worker gain from his toil? I have seen the burden God has laid on men. He has made everything beautiful in its time. He has also set eternity in the hearts of men, yet they cannot fathom what God has done from beginning to end. I know that there is nothing better for men than to be happy and do good while they live. That everyone may eat and drink and find satisfaction in his toil – this is the gift of God."*

Soon the child was caught in a new set of circumstances. The father would pick them up and then go get the mother, who had to work late. At times the children sat in the car as the father went to get a "quick beer"! These interruptions in the children's schedule lasted fifteen minutes to sometimes over an hour. So was there a solution to this problem?

Soon there was enough money for a second car. The mom had been promoted to management, so her hours were going to be longer most of the time.

The father was drinking a lot, and there were usually fights when the mother finally got home. The kids went to their rooms or sat frozen on the sofa watching the violent outbursts by the parents.

Proverbs 20:1 "Wine is a mocker and beer a brawler; whoever is led astray by them is not wise."

Ephesians 5:18 "Do not get drunk on wine which leads to debauchery. Instead be filled with the spirit."

One night the mom came home after a long, tough day at work, and the dad was drunk. The kids headed for their rooms, and the yelling began with a new vengeance. After about five or ten minutes, the boy heard the front door slam and ran to the front window to see his mom in the big Plymouth sedan, burning rubber literally down the street, like she was escaping an approaching tornado!

The boy went to the kitchen to ask his dad a question. "Dad, is Mom coming back"? His dad said, "Go to your room!" The boy replied, "But what about dinner?" He soon learned that was enough questions.

One evening, with his sister being somewhere else, his dad said, "Let's go for a ride!" The boy was car crazy already, and his dad was building him a go-cart. Soon they arrived at a tavern, and his dad said, "I'll be back. Just sit here." The boy was familiar with this situation — he had been here too many times.

Doctor visits were extremely scary for the young boy due to things happening in the exam room that the boy tried to block out of his mind. The doctor his mother had chosen was a pediatric physician specializing in boys. Later his sister would tell him about a mass of lawsuits putting the doctor out of business and lasting until his death. The boy remembers prostrate exams at age ten, but most of it he can't remember. Sexual problems would follow him most of his life!

Well finally mom and dad had a better idea about leaving the children during the day. During the school year, the father's mother, now retired, would be babysitting and doing housework to relieve the mom from those duties after her seeming-longer workdays.

Grandma went home on Friday nights after preparing dinner, another help for the boy's mom. So grandma had the weekend to rest up. The dad would take the boy on Sunday night to pick up grandma, and he found himself sitting in the car watching grandma and his dad drinking as the rain poured down at the corner bar by her apartment building.

One Sunday night etched into the boy's mind was particularly scary. As soon as the boy arrived home, Mom said, "Take a bath and go to bed." So as the boy took a bath and washed his hair, grandma came in the bathroom. Seeing the boy with his head full of soap, she dumped her coffee cup filled with hot water and tried to pour it over the boy's head. She was a wee bit tipsy still and had scalding-hot water from the tap. The boy jumped to his feet and screamed loudly until mom came in with dad. So now the whole family was in the bathroom with the boy screaming and standing in the tub naked.

The neighbor boys were younger and looked up to the boy, so he included them in his playtime. Today it was cowboys and Indians trying to sneak up on the neighbors in the back yard, but soon the neighbors went into their house. The boy had to think fast, so he said, "Let's build a campfire." Yes, you guessed it. A small brush-and-grass fire was started, the fire department was called, and the kids' parents were notified. It was not a good day for the boy or his neighborhood friends.

One day grandma and the boy were arguing about what he couldn't remember. He had not really heard much of what grandma was saying until at the final sentence, she said, "You are not part of this family. I don't know where you came from. You must be adopted." Now another burden for the boy to carry, and the boy learned not to talk about these things because it usually got him in trouble.

> *Ephesians 6:4 "Do not exasperate your children; instead bring them up in the training and instruction of the Lord."*

Then came the day when grandma found his sister in the garage hiding when she was supposed to be in school. Seems this was her regular pattern because she didn't like school.

Mom and dad came home and, after being apprised of the daughter's truant behavior, called the boy into the kitchen. After explaining that mom and dad *had to go to work*, the boy was assigned the task of taking his sister into her class and turning her over to her teacher. Then he could go to his classroom.

So Parenting 101 by a fifth grader was a new assignment. His sister was historically frightened of school. She screamed "no, no, no" and cried as if someone had killed her cat. The boy was actually pulling her down the hallway, and, of course, hardly anyone noticed...ha ha! The boy went into this to be strong but now was crying and saying he was sorry the closer they came to her classroom. It wasn't easy, but soon the sister's teacher had her, and the boy headed to his classroom crying. Upon arrival everyone looked at him and said "Is he alright"? "Sure," the boy said and took his seat.

Grade school was filled with poor choices and bad experiences for the boy — cigarettes, fights, and trying to find an identity somewhere in it all.

Other experiences included a paper route, Little League, his first bike, and driving the family Volkswagen with his dad in his uncle's wheat field. In baseball the boy found a control position: pitcher! He was good. He struck out lots of players, but just as he reached a pinnacle of success, he was traded to a Babe Ruth team with older players. He played right field. When he asked about pitching, they informed him the coach's son was their pitcher. The boy was confused. "*So why am I here,*" he wondered to himself. In a few months, he lost interest and quit. His grandfather's death happened a few weeks before. The boy couldn't deal with all that came at him. High school was coming soon.

Most people face challenging circumstances, crises, worries, and seemingly impossible situations in life.

> *Philippians 4:13 "I can do all things through Christ who gives me strength."*

High school was hard: more people, bigger class sizes, bigger school, and bigger problems. Who to turn to for friendship in a mass of kids from many different grade schools? The boy tried to run with his own school buddies, but some were moving up to a different clique to be in a better social position.

The boy had to take required classes. Didn't sound like a choice to him. Students were picked on, especially freshmen by the juniors and seniors. Math was really algebra, and it was tough. English class was taught by a gym teacher who was very tough. Can you say pop quiz? These were ten percent of your grade, so did there seem to be pressure or was it just the boy's imagination?

The boy soon found bright spots in swimming, mechanical/architectural drafting, and typing (not really). Typing was graded by a teacher who said one mistake took ten words off your actual words per minute. So go fast, but not so fast that you make mistakes and get a D on every test. English — D also. Can you say pop quiz?

Then more fun: Guidance counselors who direct you on your path to college. Only problem, with four C's and two D's as a freshman, the boy felt passed over.

Psalm 119:105 "Your word is a lamp to my feet and light for my path."

Psalm 23 "The Lord is my Shepard, I shall not want. He make me lie down in green pastures, He leads me beside quiet waters, He restores my soul. He guides me in paths of righteousness for His name's sake."

Sophomore year was Latin. The boy was put into this class by his parents. Does pharmacist sound funny, or is it just me? Yes, you guessed it: D. But A in English. Of course it was a B-English class for people having trouble. Lots of athletes in this class. Drafting was a B, so that was going well. The boy just plain liked to draw. The counselor heard this, and junior year he suggested the boy take an art class! The art teacher was a great teacher and inspired the boy's creativity. In a school challenge by a veteran's group, the ones who sell the little, red poppies to raise money, the boy came in the top five selected posters to be displayed in the hall. The boy was excited and dreamed of being an artist (remember, he loved to draw), but the family fluffed it over, just wanting to know the grade.

Moments in our lives, a chance to change course and pursue new avenues of interests. Do not let these pass by without mediating on them and discussing the situation with others.

Psalm 32:8 "I will instruct you and teach you in the way you should go; I will counsel you and watch over you."

Psalm 37:23 "If the Lord delights in a man's way, He will make his steps firm; though he may stumble, he will not fall for the Lord upholds him with His hand."

Senior year arrived in his life, and the boy had a five-class schedule, so he could work after school in a warehouse unloading railcars and sorting boxes of merchandise. His parents bought him a car to go to work and school. Soon all seniors were required to be at an assembly in the auditorium. Seems the administration was about to lay down the rules about the annual water battle that occurred outside the classrooms, in the halls, cafeteria, and on the surrounding grounds of the school. A zero-tolerance rule was going to be presented by the vice president of discipline. Soon everyone was seated, many even in the balcony. The policy was presented; any water-producing device or water balloon or any water period meant you would not graduate with the senior class. You would be required to wash lockers for three weeks and then receive your diploma of graduation. After about a twenty-minute speech, something caught the boy's peripheral vision to his right. He looked but couldn't believe it. It was a long, 1½-foot water balloon flying toward the stage. The vice president didn't see it. It looked like it would hit him or the podium he was standing behind. Then it hit — four feet to the right on the stage, spraying the V.P. with water, but just on his pants. But then the thing that happened next was unbelievable to the boy. Everyone jumped up cheering, heading for the exits. The boy said to a friend, "What a way to start the annual senior water fight!"

Needless to say, two weeks later he was outside chasing someone with a water gun, and a pair of teachers caught the boy and the others. So it was suspension first and then no graduation ceremony. Then three weeks of locker washing after school was over. Now what?

The boy's parents were mad he couldn't graduate with his classmates and he had to wash lockers for three weeks, all over a squirt gun.

> *Psalm 54:6-7 "I will praise your name, oh Lord, for it is good. For He has delivered me from all my troubles."*

Washing lockers was about as exciting as it sounds, but the janitors had to check them as the boys did them, so they had to be done right. So the boy pondered his situation — *I'll bet no one I ever run into will have received his diploma from a janitor* — and that is exactly the way it happened.

The boy met a girl, and they became lovers, and everything seemed to be going great. They decided to get married and start a family. They both had jobs, so it looked pretty good, and they decided to do it. The boy's mother had about a twenty-minute talk with him to be sure he wanted to do this marriage. The boy said yes, and the plans were made. A church was selected where the girl's mother was a part-time parishioner.

Marriage was great. The boy was ready to build a family and future.

They found an apartment in the upstairs of a remodeled 1920s house. The good news was it was affordable for the new couple's budget. The bad news was, don't take long walks in any room because the pitch of the roof took up about three feet from the wall in a couple of rooms. The bathroom was something else for the six-foot-two-inch boy, but they managed alright. Was it marital bliss? Yes, it was great for about six months.

> *Proverbs 18:22 "He who finds a wife finds what is good and receives favor from the Lord."*

> *Proverbs 5:18 "And may you rejoice in the wife of your youth."*

The boy had his nineteenth birthday, and his friends were disappearing into the draft. The boy needed a plan. After investigating on the phone with his friends, he discovered draft papers would arrive six months after his nineteenth birthday. Then he found out everyone was going into the army, except for some who were picked for the marines.

A friend said he went to the navy recruiter and got in with a great job. The only drawback: You had to enlist for four years. Yikes! That seemed like a long time to leave his family.

By the fifth month after his birthday, he had talked to his dad and mom, one of his uncles, and some more friends. As one of them told him, "If you go in the army or marines, you're going to Vietnam." It was 1968!

So he went to the navy recruiter, and the recruiter said he could get him into the supply division if he just passed the physical. The boy bought a newer car: a '66 Chevy II, Vette motor, four-speed, and, of course, two-door hardtop! His wife was taking him downtown to his physical. His physical lasted three to four hours. By the time he was done, he was tired. He called his wife from a pay phone, and she said she couldn't come and get him "Why"? he said. "Just get in the car and come and get me." She said no, she was sending one of his friends.

Why would she not drive the car? The boy remembered that in the car he had, the gas gauge was broken. She probably thought it was going to run out of gas. Well that was good. He didn't want to run out of gas on the way home. So his friend arrived, and the boy asked him, "Was it the gas gauge?" "That was part of it," his friend said. "What do you mean, part of it?" The boy was really confused. His friend said, "You'll see." They soon pulled up to the street by the apartment. He finally saw the car. The right-front wheel was bent at about a thirty-degree angle, and the fender and bumper were smashed.

So the boy confronted his wife. "What happened?" he asked as calmly as he could at the moment. Long story short, she and her girlfriend were racing people around town. "Yes, go on," he said. Well they thought the boy would notice the missing gas even though the gas gauge was broken, so they pulled into a gas station, not quite turning sharply enough with maybe a touch too much speed and hit the six-inch, steel-wrapped concrete column guarding the gas pumps. But that was all! "My new car and I just enlisted for four years in the navy," he said like it was forever.

He found a body shop close by and had them give him an estimate. Frame was bent, front suspension needed to be replaced. It was more than he paid for the car. The wife was covered on the insurance. The boy asked for mercy from the body shop, saying he had just enlisted in the navy for four years. The body shop guy said he understood and would get back with a new estimate. It was a lot lower. The car was fixed, but the body shop guy said, "My advice is sell it." So the boy did just that.

He and his wife bought a new Volkswagen, and he found out his supply school was in San Diego, and it was about four months long. So they packed up the Bug and left for San Diego right after boot camp. Four months of real fun.

Chapter Two

San Diego was a total change from Portland. It was California. More people. Close to the ocean. They found a one-bedroom apartment owned by a retired navy guy. He said sixty-five dollars a month would be all he would ask of the boy.

> *Proverbs 19:22 "Many are the plans in a man's heart, but it is the Lord's purpose that prevails."*
>
> *Proverbs 20:24 "A man's steps are directed by the Lord."*

The boy's paycheck from the navy was small because the navy required a hundred dollars be taken out and mailed to his wife. He was living with her in the same apartment, but the navy said these were the rules!

Shopping at the PX was fun — low, low, low prices! So they stocked up.

His wife got a babysitting job in the daytime: *five kids* plus *cleaning the house* and doing *all the ironing*! But it paid pretty good, so they managed.

One day his wife called and said the refrigerator died, but the landlord said, "No problem", and by that night, they had a brand-new Sears refrigerator. His landlord and his wife transferred everything out of the old one to the new one.

One day his wife picked him up and told him a funny story. She had been ironing like crazy, and she had heard two of the small kids laughing and screaming in the back yard. Time to take a peek and see what's going on. As she looked, both boys were standing on the patio, and the garden shed door was open. They were nonchalantly pouring gallons of paint over each other's heads. She stopped them right away and looked at the paint cans. "Oh no. Oil-based paint!" She called their mother, who was not very surprised, and she said there was a gallon of turpentine in the shed also. The boy's wife said that using it on their skin would not be good even if it was flushed with water afterwards. Their mom said, "It's okay. Just throw their clothes away."

Time went slipping away, and so it was December, and the boy's parents were driving down with his sister for Christmas. A Christmas celebration was planned, and the boy's wife and sister went to get a tree. It was Christmas Eve. They stopped by a parking-lot tree place with a trailer in the corner. Soon a scruffy looking man came out, and they asked about a tree. He said he only had a couple left and showed them a seven-foot monster and a little, scraggly tree with hardly any limbs of needles left on it. He said the little one was twenty-five dollars! The boy's wife and his sister said it was Christmas Eve, and the boy's sister said, "We'll give you ten dollars." The man replied, "I'd burn it right here in front of you rather than take ten dollars." The boy's sister said, "Yeah, right." The man calmly walked to his trailer and came out with a food or soup can, doused the tree with lantern fuel, and lit it on fire. Merry Christmas San Diego style, I guess.

So no tree, but naval orders were coming next week, so the next adventure would be way more exciting than this one. They all sat down to Christmas dinner and to open presents, and then the parents drove back to Portland.

Next week arrived, and names were called out in the class of twenty-five or so, and orders were read. The supply chief teaching the class would give some of his sixteen-year insight into each place the orders sent people. "London, England: clothing allowance, due to some restriction. No uniforms, only civilian clothes could be worn." Spain, Ireland submarine base, Seattle submarine base, and all kinds of ship assignments. Finally it was down to the boy and one other sailor. The chief said simply, "Naval base on land in Danang, Vietnam." The blood drained from the boy's face.

He had done everything he could not to go to Vietnam, and he and the other boy, out of twenty-five-plus people, got Vietnam. The chief said, "I have good news for you guys. You get thirty-days leave before you go to the war zone, and you'll receive sixty-five dollars a month combat pay."

Now the boy was really feeling sick. Oh yeah, it was a war zone, and they pay combat pay because there is combat. How was he going to tell his wife?

How was he going to tell his parents? But the boy thought back to the time his sister got her braces and all she did was cry. Nothing anybody said would stop the crying. The boy's mom, out of the blue, said, "Will you talk to her?" The boy said, "Me?" But he did amazingly well. She stopped crying and felt better. But Vietnam might be a little tougher.

> *Deuteronomy 24:5 "If a man has recently married, he must not be sent to war or have any other duty laid on him. For one year he is free to stay at home and bring happiness to his wife he has married."*

> *Ecclesiastes 8:8 "As no one is discharged in time of war, so wickedness will not release those who practice it."*

Well the boy and his wife drove home, for the thirty days of leave had already started. His parents were upset about Vietnam; the orders said thirteen months at a naval base outside Danang.

Many relatives were eager to give advice to the boy, but he wanted to spend time, quality time, with his wife. Thirty days passed slowly at first and then seemed to pick up speed. The boy was flying a commercial airline, contracted by the Pentagon, for a multistop trip to Vietnam. The plane had stewardesses and food and drink, the orders proclaimed!

Soon it was time to go to the airport and fly to Los Angeles and then a helicopter ride to San Bernardino, the departure point. The airport was pretty much what the boy expected. His mom, sister, and wife cried and hugged him a bunch. What the boy didn't see coming was, right as he was about to board, his dad came up, shook his hand, hugged him, and started to cry. This was a first, and the boy wiped his eyes as he realized why his dad was crying. *He might not see me again.* I mean, it's war!

The trip from Los Angeles to San Bernardino in the helicopter was white-knuckle all the way. The chopper would hit air pockets and lose about ten or twenty feet of altitude. Made the boy's stomach feel funny.

They left the United States at night, and after a forever flight, they arrived in Vietnam in the daytime. What a totally different setting. The boy had read about the French and their experience in this country, but it was way different. Vast poor areas with houses made from corrugated metal, wood, or cardboard.

Then, in contrast, upper-class people in nice, structural-type homes, along with city buildings built with walls around them. Barbwire or razor wire was like tinsel glistening in the sunlight.

Bicycles and motorbikes filled the streets with all kinds of weird-looking cards. Plus people, yes people, all over the street. People going this way and that. Women, children, but not so many men. Where are the men? Oh, the boy forgot, probably in the army.

Since the boy was the lowest rank in the navy, he figured he would be sweeping, stacking, loading, or unloading supplies. I mean, he was in the supply division.

The bus, a navy gray bus, would take us to the navy base. It was about a forty-minute ride. The base sat at the base of some mountain with a river separating the land masses: the main city on one side and the naval base and deep-water piers near the point of the land mass at the entrance into Danang Harbor.

As he rode, he gazed out his window and saw stark poverty and slums of pieced-together houses. One room, maybe two. But did they sleep on the ground? One thing was for certain, the little kids were like kids everywhere. They were outside for one thing: having fun. Many chased each other and threw stuff, and yet some just stood there, almost motionless, watching the road filled with military, civilian, and commercial construction vehicles.

Finally the bus pulled into the base. The barracks were two-story and screened in with fans. But the boy was also seeing old French, one-story barracks. Man was it warm and humid after getting off the bus. Sure enough, the old French barracks were where he was going. He got a base map and dispensary (first aid), and there was a movie theater, enlisted men's club (bar), chow hall, and various offices of those in charge.

The boy was really concerned about where he was going to work, especially in this heat and humidity. Everyone was given olive, drab uniforms. Your name and rank would be sewn on by the dry-cleaning girls (but it was dry cleaning). They dipped the uniforms in something white and milky and then ironed them so they came back like plywood. They even cracked when you unfolded them.

A slip of paper was given to the boy showing him that he was to get a ride in a pickup truck to his place of work. A caution note was also listed. "It is in Downtown Danang, right on the river, and you will be inspected each morning. This is also where the admiral works." The boy froze. They have given him someone else's orders who obviously is of a higher rank. So the boy started asking questions. Turns out it's a 1970s French foreign-legion-type fort taking up about a half of a block. Inside was the cargo operations command center. Nothing moves by boat without this unit setting it all up.

So this place must be pretty dirty if I am going to sweep it all day long, the boy pondered in his mind. Turns out, after arriving for the first day of work, he was going to be a trainee as a port coordinator. No way! Yes, it was true. Air-conditioned offices and shipping naval, army, marine, Korean, and Vietnamese army supplies and commercial construction materials. To the boy, this sounded great. It was going to be fun. And then someone, a lieutenant during orientation, said that because this was a war zone, all rate improvement waiting times had been shortened to thirty days. This meant the boy could go from E-1 to E-5 in six months. A lot of sailors spent five years or more waiting to achieve that rate. It was also five steps up in pay. All the boy could say was wow!

> *Jeremiah 29:1 1-12 "For I know the plans I have for you declares the Lord, plans to prosper you and not to harm you, plans to give you hope and a future! Then you will call upon me and come and pray to me and I will listen to you."*

Soon the boy was climbing up the rate ladder every thirty days. The commander of the unit told the boy he had some extra duty for him. The boy jumped at it enthusiastically. The commander needed to go to the various cargo-loading ramps and positions along the river and in the bay where the big ocean ships came to load and unload. So what was the boy going to do? Drive the seventeen-foot Boston Whaler with a big outboard on it. Wow!

The boy, being cautious, tried going slow since the commander was older. But almost immediately, the commander said, "Open her up. Full throttle." The boy tucked his hat down tight on his head and said, "Yes, sir!"' Soon he and the commander were *both* having fun.

A few more months, and the boy was E-5 — the maximum possible rank he could attain. He had been in the navy nine months. The officer in charge, a lieutenant with an Ivy League degree and an Annapolis graduate, called the boy into his office. The boy thought he had done something wrong but really couldn't think what it could be for the life of him.

The lieutenant started off by congratulating the boy on quickly moving up rank to E-5 storekeeper 2nd class. The boy said, "Thank you," and that he worked hard achieving it. The lieutenant then commented that the boy had been at various shipping-port desks asking questions and writing down each one's individual characteristics. The boy said yes, he wanted to be in charge of the whole enlisted men's group of workers.

The lieutenant then shocked the boy by saying, "All this has moved me to nominate you as a war-zone promotion to the Annapolis Naval Academy." The boy thought of what to say but no thoughts came except, "Thank you, sir."

New barracks were being built across the road from the base and were finally finished. The boy was about to move out from the old French barracks to the new one almost immediately. He was double bunked, so he took the top one, and time continued to pass.

People were talking about the Tet Offensive. The boy had seen it in his morning messaging he received, for he was now the person in charge of the night crew. Since the war was twenty-four hours a day, two crews were required to move all the cargo. The boy had memorized the coast guard ammunition explosive classes and how to load the different kinds of ammunition, dynamite, and cannon shells aboard the boats moving it to the various ports.

The vehicle was called U boats. They had a tower at the back to see over the load and a twelve-foot high bow that dropped a ramp so a rough-terrain, large forklift could load the material.

One evening they came to the old French fort by the river, and security and extra guards were projecting a new presence at the front gate. As he got upstairs, he noticed a piece of plywood over the lieutenant's office window. When he walked into the office, the mood was somber. An explosion had happened at the cement plant half a mile away, and the concussion blew out a bunch of windows. The lieutenant had just gotten up to get a cup of coffee or he would have been sprayed with thousands of glass shards, now stuck in the wall across from the window. No, it was not safety glass. This was 1930s regular glass.

A week later, the boy, riding in the truck to the French fort office, was being delayed. There was a terrific explosion but muffled. They soon saw what the problem was. In front of them, a U boat sat at the loading ramp, but its tower part was half-submerged in the river about fifty feet from the ramp. The front half of the boat was about fifty feet clear of the water's edge, as if it had been shoved up on the asphalt by force. The driver of the truck came up to a military police checkpoint and asked what had happened. The enemy had shot a small mortar from the tall grass across the road from the ramp. It hit a case of dynamite and blew the boat in half, along with two pallets of 105mm army howitzer projectiles now lying all over the place. EOD (Explosive Ordinance Disposal) was sandbagging them and blowing them up if they were deemed too dangerous to move.

When the boy finally arrived at the French fort, he received more bad news. The lieutenant called him into his office. The boy had been rejected from the Annapolis nomination because he was married! *A funny naval rule*, the boy thought to himself.

A few weeks later, the French fort was going to be abandoned by the navy altogether due to the high value of a target with the admiral there, plus the other officers and enlisted men. They were moving to double-wide trailers set up as offices at the deep-water piers — a higher security area.

Now sleeping was fairly easy after working twelve hours, and so the boy was back to days until the move. Late one night about four hours before the sunrise, the boy sat straight up in his bunk. It was like someone threw a bucket of water on him. He looked at his watch: 2:15 A.M. He wasn't groggy or half asleep; he was more awake than ever before. Then he heard it. It sounded like the Fourth of July. The large mortars being fired. That hissing sound as they climbed in the air. The boy yelled, "Incoming," and eighty people headed from the second floor down to the bunker layered with sandbags. The attack sirens were now blowing. The boy only had made a couple of steps, and there was an explosion. It was very close. Soon everyone was in the bunker safe.

The army had triangular radar, so within thirty seconds, you could hear the full battery of cannon fire. The boy learned that their shells would land within a minute at the launch site of the mortar. People wanted to get out of the bunker to see what was happening. The boy stayed back. Then more hisses, and one fell not two hundred feet from the bunker in a sewage-pond bunker. Well that brought everyone back in quickly. Now more hisses and explosions across the road at the base where the boy used to be sleeping.

The boy talked to others who had been there. They moved just in time, but what about those who were there now? Waiting for the all-clear siren, it was painfully slow. The boy was talking about how he had woken up before it started, and it was strange.

Okay, all-clear siren, everybody back to bed. But the boy still thought about waking up, like wide awake, more than ever before.

He was talking to his friends. "Why did I wake up before it started? I mean, it was minutes, and I was sitting on my bunk going, 'Why am I so awake?'" His friends said it was just a coincidence and what the boy needed was a beer at the EM club. The boy seemed to feel that it was something completely different, but he couldn't put his finger on it.

> *Acts 12:6-9 "The night before Herod was to bring Him to trial, Peter was sleeping between two soldiers, bound with chains, and sentries stood guard at the entrance. Suddenly an angel appeared in the cell. He struck Peter on the side and woke him up. 'Quick, get up,' he said and the chains fell off Peter's wrists. Then the angel said, 'Put on your clothes and sandals.' And Peter did so. 'Wrap your cloak around you and follow me,' the angel told him. Peter followed him out of prison, but he had no idea that what the angel was doing was really happening; he thought he was seeing a vision."*

Then came the day the boy received good news from home. His wife was pregnant. The baby was due to arrive right before his seven months in Vietnam, which came with a seven-day, rest-and-relaxation break. Married people could take it in Hawaii. This was all great news to the boy.

> *Psalms 127: 3-5 "Sons are a heritage from the Lord, children a reward from Him. Like arrows in the hand of a warrior are sons born in one's youth. Blessed is the man whose quiver is full of them."*

Hawaii was very nice, and the boy's wife had lived there for eight years or more. Her father still lived there, and he had offered his home so the new couple wouldn't have to spend a lot of money at an Hawaiian hotel. Seven days in what most people call tropical paradise, the family had a good time together. The new baby was just a couple months old, so they were limited where they could go.

The boy's wife's father was a different guy when he was drinking, but there were no problems, as the couple spent a lot of time by themselves. The boy tried to talk about Vietnam and his night during the rocket attack, but it was not as big a deal to everyone else as it was to the boy.

Soon time had passed, and it was time for the boy to return to Vietnam. His wife was working on getting a job and finding a babysitter as she returned home.

Now back in Vietnam, the boy was working at the deep-water piers in the double-wide trailer office. Every night a guard walking the piers would toss concussion grenades into the water to dispel enemy swimmers. The bang could even be heard in the office where the boy was working. Just another reminder of the war zone they were still living in day and night.

Now everyone was talking about getting short. This was not about shrinking in size but in time — the less time you had left. The days counted until leaving the country of Vietnam was what was called being "short" or "a short-timer." If they only knew what kind of a country they were going back to, they might not have said so much about it!

They boy found out from people who had left ahead of him that San Bernardino was a bottleneck you wanted to avoid. Why? Because it delayed the forty-minute-or-so drive to LAX to catch your flight home and another thirty days of leave. The boy decided to ship most of his stuff home so he would only be carrying one bag when going through customs.

Soon a medal ceremony was scheduled, and the boy learned his unit had received a unit citation for performance. He was also going to receive a Vietnam campaign medal and a couple others. So it was, on a hot and humid day, many stood at attention in dress-white uniforms, and medals were pinned on, and handshakes were given, along with paperwork documenting the ceremony.

Soon it was thirty days to go, then twenty, then ten, then five, and then it was only one. The boy was leaving Vietnam unscathed and properly rewarded in rank and medals for his good job. Finally he got his orders for where he was headed after his thirty days of leave. The boy could hardly believe his eyes as he read the words. After spending thirteen months on the ground, he was going to a be on a missile destroyer that was coming to Vietnam. At least he would be floating offshore!

> *Psalm 25:20-21 "Guard my life and rescue me; let me not be put to shame, for I take refuge in you. May integrity and uprightness protect me, because my hope is in you."*

The boy's thirty days of vacation was a definite refreshing period. The stress of Vietnam passed as the boy realized his rank as an E-5 2nd class storekeeper would put him in a supervisory position. The family, his parents, and others wrote letters to the Oregon congressmen about having a young, new father having to go back to Vietnam. Soon a letter came for the boy from one of the congressmen. It was three pages long and basically said, "I can't help you." The boy was working for the country. But the country had no mercy and compassion.

> *Exodus 33:19 "I will have mercy on whom I will have mercy and I will have compassion on whom I will have compassion."*

So the boy was catching the ship in San Diego, where it was departing from for its Vietnam tour. The airplane ride was long with a stopover. Soon the boy was walking up the gangway to the ship. It was big, with two 5 x 54 gun mounts fore and aft. It also had air-defense missiles and antisubmarine misses at midships.

The boy was sent to the XO (executive officer), the number two to the captain. He shook the boy's hand and introduced himself. The boy was eager to find out where he would be assigned.

The X's first words were, "So I see you didn't want to come be on our ship". The boy was shocked. "Why do you say that"? said the boy dumbfoundedly. "Well it's pretty simple," said the XO. "I have all your relatives' letters to your congressman right in your file here."

The boy had no response. He was frozen with fear. Finally he said that he had just spent thirteen months on the ground in Danang. "I see that also in your file," the XO said.

So the boy was to be the main supervisor at central storeroom, where people came to get parts for all the ship's components. He would have two seamen under him to go fetch the parts, put away new stock, and do inventory. So it wasn't exactly terrible.

The boy got back into shipboard activity and, as a supervisor, didn't do a lot of lifting and sweeping. He just delegated.

Chapter Three

Just before they were about to leave for Vietnam one morning while awaiting colors (the raising of the flag), everyone was pointing to something floating in the water about forty feet away from the ship. A tugboat was coming along at a slow speed, and they got its attention, so it slowed to a stop. The tug boat had a long hook, and it hooked the object with a pole and brought it close. It was a sailor in dress blues with a peacoat (all wool). They pulled him aboard dead!

People were dying in Vietnam, a war zone, and here's a guy who just fell in the water and drowned. Wow, everyone was shocked!

Battle stations! All hands, man your battle stations. The boy's station was in the engineering office, a cool spot. All drills were introduced at this point, and the rest of the ship had to react. Some atomic attacks, submarine plots, and missiles fired at the ship. Next stop: San Clemente Island gunnery and missile range. Targets were floated by a towing ship, and the guns fired a five-inch shell about two feet long with a three-foot powder charge behind it. The guns were the primary defense of the ship.

The rockets or missiles for planes attacking the ship were made by a tire company. The guns were always on in case they didn't go where directed. We fired some at some drones, but the boy didn't get the results.

Next stop Hawaii, and the boy had been there, so it was only two days and back into the water. The trip lasted about three to four weeks, and they were in Vietnam.

The ship did some patrols in the southernmost part of Vietnam, known as the Delta. It is really a dangerous thing to put this big of a ship in a sixty-to-eighty-foot-wide waterway. Soon it became not so exciting except for turning around in wide, lake-type areas. Before you could say, "We're done," we were!

New assignment: gunfire liaison within a short distance of the DMA (demilitarized zone), an area separating North and South Vietnam.

Supplies and troops would come down the Ho Chi Minh Trail, which really was a network of routes. Most of the supplies came by cart or truck or even people carrying the smaller loads. America was smart. A small, camouflaged item about as big as a silver dollar was dropped by U.S. planes all over certain areas. These electronic bugs were sensitive to people moving and could be monitored in real time. So when they signaled people moving, bombing missions were assigned. But if no planes were available, the army's naval gunfire liaison officer would plot target points and ask for three rounds of HE (high explosive) at each target point.

So this is what the ship was assigned to do — fifty to one hundred points or more a night. This is when the enemy moved so satellites or high-flying reconnaissance planes could not take pictures. But they had infrared photo equipment also.

To shoot that many shells required resupply frequently — fifty or so projectiles in a pallet and three-foot-long canisters of powder separately. They would arrive at mid-ship, third deck, but had to be put in the magazine four decks down. To do this required manpower, like a bucket brigade. Take one sixty-pound projectile, pass it, and turn to receive the next one from the guy next to you. Now ladder-type stairs separated decks, so these areas required up and down passing of projectiles. This is where people could only last maybe ten or fifteen minutes.

So what happens? They are low on ammunition for the big guns, so they go to the resupply ship sitting well-offshore.

Both ships match speed about seventy-five feet apart. Then through an exchanges of ropes, a block-and-tackle type of setup is put into place.

So what kind of weather do they do this in? Leftovers from a typhoon, high seas, high winds — and they're handling stuff that explodes!

Well it actually almost came off without a problem. But as they started to pull away from the resupply ship, the XO put too much rudder into the turn. This caused the ship to list badly to starboard (the right side of the ship), and a pallet of shells slid across the deck, knocking a young sailor over a three-foot cable railing, and then the pallet of fifty projectiles went to pieces, dropping into the sea right where the young sailor had fallen in. People feared the projectiles would snag the boy's clothes and take him to the bottom of the sea.

But the young sailor had someone watching over him. His life jacket brought him almost immediately to the surface. But the rear of the ship was swinging into him, and that's ten-foot propellers pushing the boat through the water!

Now in close quarters, ships had screw guards: large, metal tubing welded to the side of the ship in half-moon shapes to bump other vessels so they wouldn't get too close to the propellers. The young sailor, now floating, bobbed up and smacked his head on the screw guard.

Meanwhile man-overboard quarters was called, and each division of the ship had a specific place to meet so a roll call could be taken.

Amidst this calamity, the boy still had a sixty-pound projectile in his hand to pass to the next guy. Then he could go to the supply division assembly area for a roll to be taken.

So again the boy saw a near-death experience happen on his ship. But soon the young sailor in the ocean with very poisonous sea snakes was picked up, still floating in his life jacket.

> *Job 25:5-6 "The dead are in deep anguish, those beneath the waters and all that live in them. Death is taken before God, destruction lies uncovered."*

> *Psalm 89:48 "What man can live and not see death, or save himself from the power of the grave!"*

Night after night, boom, boom, boom! Three projectiles heading for a target point. A really funny and scary thing happened one night while firing. Target coordinates punched into the computer, the big gun aimed itself, but it's not a perfect system. The officer of the watch had to stand on the bridge overlooking the gun, and his duty was to say, "looks good," after each new coordinate was entered into the computer. So after fifty, seventy-five or one hundred targets, everyone gets a little lax. So the new coordinate was entered, and the boy and his friends were on the signal bridge, a deck higher, taking pictures of the gun shooting. The gunnery officer asks, "Looks good?" The officer of the watch says, "Yes," but the gun is pointing straight up in the air. So everybody yells, "No sir, look," and he quickly stops the gunnery boys from firing.

This could have been disastrous. The ship could have sunk itself. How about that headline? Night after night, this firing got old quick. It's too noisy to sleep, and you're not really ready to sleep after being up for twelve hours at a time.

So the boy and his friend made it to the back of the ship, as far away from the front gun as possible. Again a new, unique experience happens.

A helicopter is flying over a piece of land that sticks out about a quarter of a mile into the ocean to the east. This is close to, if not the DMZ. Suddenly the boy pulls up his camera. Red tracer bullets are flying up at the helicopter from the ground. It looks like red dashes someone is painting. Soon the helicopter comes back after making a small circle to get away from the firing. Now multiple red dashes come up from the jungle, and the helicopter returns fire. The helicopter is equipped with a 60,000-rounds-a-minute electric Gatling mini gun. No dashes though — it looks like someone is pouring red paint out of the helicopter, a solid stream that hits the ground and splashes everywhere. Soon red dashes come from the jungle again. The helicopter goes out over the ocean. The boy's friends say, "Did you get that on film"? The boy replied, "Yes, five or six shots."

Then it got strangely quiet. You could not hear the helicopter anymore. Then suddenly the piece of land exploded into fire, and you could hear an F4 jet powering up out of a dive. Thirty seconds passed. Another explosion — of fire — and another F4 jet had dropped napalm. The jungle burned, and the boy kept on taking pictures. It was nighttime. He thought, *these are going to be great!*

As the boy lay in his bunk later trying to get to sleep, he was calculating the cost. How many enemy: three to five maximum. The cost of the helicopter: a half million — the gun, the three- or two-man crew. Then two F4 jets, twenty-five to thirty million. Couple of napalm bombs: twenty to fifty or sixty thousand. For three or five people! It was overkill. War was stupid. A waste of young talent and massive tax-money spending.

The ship was developing an electrical problem with its generators. They were going to have to go to the Philippines for repairs. Parts were ordered from the States. It sounded like we were going to be there a while.

So the boy wondered where he was going to next after the Philippines. After extensive repairs that took a while, the ship was assigned as carrier escort. This would be a totally new adventure.

As the ship arrived into the carrier group, there were multiple ships doing or responsible for different tasks. The boy's ship was responsible for pickup of pilots who had to ditch their aircraft in the water because it was too damaged to land safely.

The best thing was flybys or buzzing the escorts. Two F4s, one-to-one, flying in formation about a hundred feet off the ocean, going as fast as allowed, the boy guesses, but wow, what pictures. They were anticipating returning to the States, but an offer of something else came along: a side trip of two weeks in Australia. The ship's crew had to vote for home or Australia. The boy wanted Australia bad. But the majority voted for home.

> *Deuteronomy 20:5 "The officers will say to the army:*
> *20:7 has anyone become pledged to a woman and not married her? Let him go home, or he may die in battle and someone else marry her."*
> *20:8 "then the officers shall add; is any man afraid or faint-hearted? Let him go home so that his brothers will not become disheartened too."*

The voyage home was great! Good weather most of the way and stops in Singapore, Midway, Hawaii, and Hong Kong. Hong Kong was a shopping capital because of its low prices on electronics, motorcycles, and various other items. The boy thought the pink Volkswagen bus that came to the pier where the ship was docked with Australian and British ships was pretty cool. Authentic British fish 'n' chips. Warm evenings and cool breezes off the sea made the atmosphere perfect for a great meal after a hard day's work.

The fish 'n' chips were cooked while you waited — then malt vinegar splashed, a handful of salt, and then wrapped in newspaper. Perfect!

The boy had the opportunity to go to a restaurant that served Kobe beef — tender, melt-in-your-mouth steaks. A group also headed for a Hong Kong hot spot where you could have a five-course meal for under fifteen dollars a person, including baked Alaska for dessert.

The boy found out the ship would be stationed at Treasure Island in San Francisco for a complete retrofit. They basically update just about everything, so much so that the crew must be put ashore in multilevel barracks. This stay would last right up to the boy's three-year anniversary of enlistment. So he was anxious for new orders somewhere close for his final year.

Working on the ship during the day and going to see San Francisco at night was the routine throughout their stay at Treasure Island.

Soon orders arrived for the boy. He would be stationed at a naval bombing range in Boardman, Oregon, about two hundred miles east of Portland.

The best news, however, was he could have his wife and new son with him and did not have to live on the base. It was also more money because of that fact — no living quarters on the base.

The boy would be a supply officer, enlisted, of course, with no helpers or people to supervise. All requisitions had to go through the army supply center at Umatilla Army depot, a depot for chemical weapons.

The boy would have to drive there about fifteen miles from the naval bombing range. The work was amazingly easy compared to what he had been doing, so he enjoyed his time with his family. His son was growing like crazy, and the boy and his wife tried to plan their lives after the navy.

The home was a ten-foot-wide, fifty-foot-long trailer house that was a bargain for rent. The only thing that scared his wife and son was the thunderstorms in the summertime that rose up in the desert area where the base was located. So the lightning flashed and thunder boomed, rattling the trailer house and scaring his wife and son terribly. Then the great hailstorm would come pounding the trailer like a drum.

> *Job 37:3-4 "He unleashed his lightning beneath the whole heaven and sends it to the ends of the earth."*

> *Job 36:32-33 "He fills His hands with lightning and commands it to strike its mark. His thunder announces the coming storm; even the cattle make know its approach."*

> *Revelation 11:19 "Then God's temple in heaven was opened, and within his temple was seen the ark of his covenant. And there came flashes of lightning, rumblings, peals of thunder, an earthquake and great hailstorm."*

Then came the day of decision: the navy's reenlistment offer. An electronics tech, nuclear, had been on submarines and was offered eighteen thousand dollars for a six-year reenlistment. The boy thought, *It has not been a bad four years.* So he was at least going to consider the offer. Finally it came: six years, four thousand dollars. Why so little? It was wartime. But it was based, the boy found out, on supply and demand. There were lots of supply-division people, so the low offer to the boy. After discussing it with his wife, they decided it was better to get out. But first a crisis lay waiting just around the bend. His son suddenly got sick, and they had to take him to the hospital in Hermiston, Oregon, about forty miles up the road. The couple waited in the waiting room for the news. Finally the doctor came out. He was going to have to do surgery.

It seemed to last forever. The doctor said he would soon be in recovery, but a nurse from the operating room said that it was close, and the boy's son almost dies during the operation. He was losing so much blood. But many hands save him! The couple was relieved.

> *Exodus 13: 1-2 "The Lord said to Moses, "Consecrate to me every first born male. The first offering of every womb among the Israelites belongs to Me whether man or animal."*

Crisis averted, the boy and his wife headed for Portland. His parents told him when he arrived his grandmother could put up some money to buy them a trailer home to live in as they got settled.

The boy went back to his previous employer, who, according to federal law, was supposed to be holding his job for him with all his seniority, like he had been there working the last four years. The boy's boss had told his other workers not to worry about the boy taking one of their jobs because he was going to farm the boy out to other places in the factory. Although this was illegal and in violation of union rules, also, it was the perfect thing for the boy. These different jobs all over the factory showed the boy the entire manufacturing process, and he memorized lots of information.

After a couple of months, the boy came back to his original area and soon learned all the jobs as he did them. In a year, he was lead man over others who had worked there over twenty years. Then his boss got promoted, and the boy got his job. This was a big promotion and a big pay raise.

The boy talked to his wife about going to community college to become more valuable to the company. The GI Bill would pay for it. This brought in more money. Soon the boy's wife was pregnant again with a daughter. This was welcome news to the couple, and they looked on weekends to find a house.

Then the boy discovered Oregon had a VA loan program. This would get the couple into the home with a low down payment and low monthly payments. Now if they could just find a house.

Early one morning, the realtor called about a home in an upscale area of custom homes. This was the builder's house he lived in while building the community.

The house was on a cul-de-sac off a corner — quiet, lots of tall fir trees, and a big back yard. The boy was already planning a fenced yard for his children and patio furniture. The house had three bedrooms, two baths, a double-car garage and was only $17,500. The payments were just $235 a month. Wow, this was absolutely the perfect place for the family.

Now the boy was working ten-hour days at his job, with three classes a week at the community college at night. Long days of work and study put a real burden on the whole family. His wife was not working now with two children to take care of. The daughter was born just before they moved into the house.

Years passed, and soon another crisis faced the boy and his family. The factory was scheduled to close, and hundreds of people would lose their jobs. The plant superintendent has assured the boy that he and he only would stay to the final day, giving him six to nine months to plan a new life.

The boy was frustrated by all this, and he could see his family struggling also. The boy turned to smoking pot to escape all the pressure and the circumstances facing him.

The boy's wife said her brother in Reno said there were jobs down there and asked, "Why don't you move down?" The boy immediately thought about the house having to be sold and everyone uprooted. His relatives didn't have much to say or much advice either. The boy was perplexed and didn't know which way to turn.

7

The factory was closing. The house sold for double what the boy purchased it for, and it sold fast. This was going to be the first step in a two-year nightmare that would tear the family apart and put everyone through divorce.

Malachi 2:14, 16 "You ask 'Why?' It is because the Lord is acting as a witness between you and the wife of your youth, because you have broken faith with her though she is your partner, the wife of your marriage covenant…'I hate divorce,' says the Lord God of Israel, 'and I hate a man covering himself with violence as well as with his garment,' says the spirit, and do not break faith."

Mathew 19:3-9 "Some Pharisees came to Him to test Him. They asked, 'Is it lawful for a man to divorce his wife for any and every reason?' 'Haven't you read,' Jesus replied 'that at the beginning the Creator made them male and female and said for this reason a man will leave his father and mother and be united to his wife and the two will become on flesh. So they are no longer two but one. Therefore what God has joined together, let man not separate.' 'Why then,' they asked, 'did Moses command that a man give his wife a certificate of divorce and send her away?' Jesus replied, 'Moses permitted you to divorce your wives because your hearts were hard. But it was not this way from the beginning. I tell you that anyone who divorces his wife except for marital unfaithfulness and marries another woman commits adultery.'"

Chapter Four

Reno, Sin City, where just about everything goes. The family lived in the basement of the wife's brother while the boy looked for a job. It was 1979, and the boy applied at a national factory doing the same thing he had been doing. A vice president flew in from Massachusetts to interview the boy. After twenty minutes, he asked the boy, "You want to run this factory, don't you"? The boy said, "Yes!"

> *Proverbs 27:1 "Do not boast about tomorrow for you do not know what a day may bring forth."*
>
> *1 Corinthians 1:31 "Let Him who boasts, boast in the Lord."*
>
> *Galatians 6:14 "May I never boast except in the cross of Christ through which the world has been crucified to me, and I to the world."*

The boy had to do some training in Massachusetts and North Carolina before returning to Reno. The boy was going to run the computer system, mainly printing schedules, production stats, paychecks, and various internal reports.

The boy was being groomed for management, and everyone knew it. There were some who wanted the boy out so as to continue in their own way of doing things. The boy had learned in his management classes that people's number-one thing they hated was change.

The boy went drinking with a bunch of ladies after work and was getting too close to the people who saw a way to get promoted was to be on the boy's side.

Months passed, and the boy was now doing drugs and drinking almost every night. It was a path that led nowhere!

So the boy went out to dinner with a lady, and they really hit it off. Next the boy was having an affair, and it was going to split his family in two.

The boy was out looking for apartments. The divorce was right around the corner. The boy wanted to do what he wanted to do. If only he could see his selfish attitude. But he was blinded by his ego and pride.

> *Proverbs11:2 "When pride comes, then comes disgrace, but with humility comes wisdom."*

> *Proverbs 22:4 "Humility and the fear of the Lord bring wealth and honor and life!"*

The boy's wife was pretty much done with him, but the boy said he would rent a moving truck and drive his wife, his son, and his daughter back to Oregon.

His children didn't understand and cried at the drop of a hat. The boy could not feel their fear or pain. He only cared about himself. On the return trip on an airplane to Reno, he went to talk to a lawyer about divorce and child support.

The lawyer said he would have to act fast to beat his wife to the judge, and Reno was the capital of fast divorce.

The boy decided to return to community college in Reno to collect the last of his VA benefits. The lady that liked him moved in, and it was all fine for about three months. Shocking news came to the boy at work. The vice president, his mentor, had cancer and was going to die. Suddenly the boy felt alone, and everyone working with him could see it also.

A few months passed, and the boy heard his mentor had died. Two days later, he was fired by the factory manager. Now what was he going to do?

> *Proverbs 3:25-26 "Have no fear of sudden disaster or the ruin that overtakes the wicked. For the Lord will be confidence and will keep your foot from being snared."*

Proverbs 2:12-15 "Wisdom will save you from the ways of wicked men, from men whose words are perverse, who leave straight paths to walk in dark ways, who delight in doing wrong and rejoice in the perverseness of evil, whose paths are crooked and who are devious in their ways."

Now the boy looked to other women again — and this while he was living with this lady. Going from one to another, the boy didn't care about what he was doing and the consequences of his actions. One girl called and said she was pregnant and wanted him to help her. He was working at another job but was soon fired from there also.

The girl was going to get an abortion. She wanted money. The boy had none. He was saving to go back home, but he was going to have to doctor up his resume to get a college grad job. He only lasted two months. But he almost had the cash he needed. Then he got the phone call. It was his mother. Dad was really sick, so he should come home quickly.

The boy needed to get rid of his furniture. He gave it to someone because he had to leave. He wanted to see his dad so badly, but it wasn't to be.

Although the boy drove straight through, sleeping in rest areas for a couple of hours and then back on the road again, he was not close yet. Then it started to snow very lightly, so the boy slowed from eighty to sixty-five. Snow was real light on the road, and the sports car he was driving didn't slip a bit. Another rest stop coming up, the boy needed to stop. He pulled in, stopped, and got out of the car. He slowly started sliding with the slant of the parking lot. It was a sheet of ice. The boy was perplexed. The car was having no trouble, but he could barely stay on his feet.

Deuteronomy 4:31 "For the Lord, your God is a merciful God, he will not abandon or destroy you."

Finally the boy arrived home. His mother told him he was too late. They already had buried him. The boy was shocked! He needed to see his family, but was it too soon?

The boy took stock of all the evil and wicked things he had done to many people. He had sold drugs. He had committed adultery, lied, and lied some more. He had been abusive to people and kids. Plus he was guilty of murder of an unborn child.

How far had he fallen. He was disgusted with the whole thing. He must try to put things back together. He could do it. All he had to do was get his family back. But he needed a job first. He was going to really need a good job.

But he needed money. So his mom said, "Go see your aunt." The boy was excited about this. They were real religious people, and he felt uncomfortable around them. They were nice to talk to, and they prayed, hugged him, and told him that Jesus loved him. They gave him money.

Little did the boy know that change was planted in him when his aunt hugged him. This was not going to happen fast, but a seed was planted.

> *Jeremiah 4:22 "My people are fools. They do not know me. They are senseless children. They have no understanding. They are skilled in doing evil. They do not know how to do good."*

The boy soon found a national insurance company hiring people to work all over Oregon. Little did the boy know that this was a job especially for him. The training included prayer. It was a positive-thinking approach to all aspects of his life.

Somehow his family did want to see him. His children had grown into their teens and preteens. They were kind of standoffish at first, but then the family started doing things together and going out to dinner.

Everyone was feeling more like a family, but there was a shadowy uneasiness standing in the background.

The family wanted to move to a better area, and the boy wanted to get married again, but the big question still remained: Did his wife also want to get married again? They found a duplex about two miles away that was close to some good schools. It had three bedrooms and a nice front and back yard.

The insurance job was going pretty good. The boy had made top 4 percent in the nation one week and won an award. The car was not in too good of shape, so the boy was looking for a cheap vehicle that could carry the whole family. He found a big sedan with four doors that was a good car at a cheap price. The insurance job was more and more out of town, and the boy missed his family. He was looking for something different with less time required. After two short jobs that lasted just a couple of months, he found an international company that was tops in the construction field.

They interviewed the boy and said he would have to go to the Midwest for three weeks of training. The great news is they paid him a training salary, plus benefits for food and expenses. The bad news was it was wintertime, the middle of November, when he left with a hope for good weather. His wife had a job with an accountant, so the family was doing well financially.

> *Titus 2:6-7 "Similarly, encourage the young men to be self controlled. In everything set them an example by doing what is good."*

This job lasted for seven years. The boy, once comfortable in his position, started going back to his old ways: drinking and drugs. This caused all kinds of problems for the family. But at least they were still together.

The boy's sister said she was selling her home, and the boy jumped to buy it. His sister was anxious to build her own home. She had also been divorced and was caring for two children by herself. But she had a good job at an insurance company and was doing good things in her life.

The boy's mom was acting peculiar and doing strange things. His sister took her to the doctor, and the diagnosis was Alzheimer's disease, early stage. The care of his mother was going to require part-time caregivers and money, and thankfully his mother had some investments.

The first years of care for his mother involved construction changes to the house and investigating caregivers for the part-time care. The boy was responsible for the construction and management of the investments, plus to do his job and be with his family. It seemed to be too much to manage, but the boy took it on his own to do it all.

A conclusion of his sister and the boy was that the care people were not checked out well enough, and problems popped up. So while discussing all this on morning walks, a positive came out of this negativity. Why not start a company that did criminal checks on each caregiver and matched them specifically to the person getting the care so their interests would be as much alike as possible.

> *Philippians 2:3-4 "Do nothing out of selfish ambition or vain conceit, but in humility consider others better than yourselves. Each of you should look not only to your own interests, but also the interests of others."*

The boy's sister thought that a cleaning service based in her house would be a good start and then move into the assisted-living arena. The business took off, and the boy's wife went to work for the business also. Big clients were obtained, and the assisted-living part had some nationally famous clients also. The boy's job, however, was closing down due to a consolidation of marketing at the home office. The boy had been going to a nearby Lutheran church, taking his children with him. But his wife said she didn't want to go to church.

> *Proverbs 22:6 "Train a child in the way he should go and when he is old he will not turn from it."*

The boy was closing the company's operation in Portland, and he asked the Lord for his own company in a prayer. Now a carpet-laying company was coming to recarpet the house. He tried to negotiate the price. The first 10 percent came easy. The rest was hard work. He noted that the removal of the old carpet was a significant amount, so he said he would do it by himself. The carpet store owner was trying to talk him out of it and told him extra time and money would be charged if it was not ready when the installer arrived. So the boy asked the installer how he wanted it done. Immediately the idea flashed in his mind. He could underbid these people and make a good living. He had saved almost 40 percent on his recarpet job, so he could see plenty of room built into the first price quoted.

Then he thought about recycling. Everyone was doing it. It was a trend. If he could follow that trend, it would become a business growth avenue. He then was reading the paper and saw used carpet advertised. This could be another recycling opportunity. Additional growth. Who would need this service? Carpet stores because they could do more jobs if they were not removing also.

What he asked for, he received: a blessing from the Lord. The boy had a small pickup but would need a bigger one down the line as the business grew. The boy went out to sell the idea wherever he could find someone to listen. Now realtors were his first target and then carpet stores and property-management companies.

The boy soon learned that some people changed their carpet because they didn't like the color or the color clashed with their furniture. Some of this carpet was brand new or less than six months old. The pad under the carpet was also new. So the boy could sell the carpet and the pad to poor people who could not afford new carpet. The boy did all the work himself and realized this idea had come from God. The boy needed something more, but he could not figure out what he was missing.

Chapter Five

The boy was watching the TBN religious channel one morning, and he became enticed by what a preacher was saying. He listened more intently, and soon the preacher said, "God has a plan for your life." A plan to glory God and become a child of God's family. This all sounded good to the boy since his parents had died, along with a lot of his other relatives. He needed a new family.

The preacher said all he had to do was repent — or turn and go the other way. Confess his sins that he had committed and thank Jesus for his sacrifice for all on the cross. The preacher said the work has already been done. Jesus died for all the sin of the world. All the boy had to do was accept the offer to be reconciled to God and become a child of God's family. He thought it was too simple but thought it had to be so all could understand it.

The preacher said, "We are going to pray a prayer now telling God you're sorry for all the sin in your life."

So the boy got on his knees praying. "God, I am a sinner, and I am sorry for all the sin in my life I have done." He told of all his sins. "I repent of all these sins that Jesus took to the cross to reconcile me back to you. I thank you, God, for Jesus and his sacrifice for me on the cross. I put my faith, trust, and belief in Jesus as my Lord and Savior. Thank you, God, for sending your son to die in my place."

> *Romans 3:23 "For all have sinned and fall short of the glory of God."*

> *Romans 6:23 "For the wages of sin is death, but the gift of God is eternal life in Christ Jesus our Lord."*
>
> *Romans 10:9 "That if you confess with your mouth, 'Jesus is Lord' and believe in your heart that God raised Him from the dead, you will be saved."*
>
> *Ephesians 2:8-9 "For it is by grace you have been saved through faith and this not from yourselves, it is the gift of God, not by works, so no one can boast."*

Suddenly the boy felt totally different, like a huge burden had been lifted off his shoulders. He had this burning desire to buy a Bible, so off he went and found a study Bible, which he began to read diligently. He, in the winter months, wanted also to look for a church for the next coming Sunday. He found one six blocks away. It was perfect! Sunday he dressed in his suit and headed for church, but it was extremely icy. His four-wheel-drive truck was handling it just fine. He arrived at the church and tried to maneuver the icy parking lot without falling down. He made it to the door and went right on into the lobby. No one was there. *Maybe they started church early today,* he thought. He went into the sanctuary. Again, no one was there at all. The boy decided to pray and read his Bible by himself. It was a real personal moment for the boy, to be in God's house praying and reading his word all alone. (Later he found out everyone who showed up met in the chapel across the side of the parking lot.)

The boy now had a desire to do some volunteering to help around the church. Next he was doing communion for people unable to come to church — people in rest homes or retirement centers. He was singing in a senior choir that traveled to rest homes and retirement centers. Then he started teaching Bible study groups and even helped out in the oldest Sunday school class at times. Once in a while, he was teaching. In this class, a lady came up to him and said, "This is your gift — use it well."

Now the boy was busy going to Bible study in a home during the week and even preaching at rest homes two or three times a month now and again to fill in for others who needed time off or had other commitments.

The boy pondered all this in his heart. He had come so far from where he was back in Reno.

But things were not all great. His wife left him and wanted another divorce. The boy tried to talk to her, but she just cried and would not take his calls. It was going to end badly again. Why was this happening? There was an argument, but was that it or was it something else? The boy was already in his own apartment, and his business was now growing at a faster rate.

> *Philippians 4:6 "Don't be anxious about anything, but in everything, by prayer and petition, with thanksgiving present your request to God."*

> *Jeremiah 29:11 "For I know the plans I have for you, declares the Lord, plans to prosper you and not to harm you, plans to give you hope and a future."*

The boy needed a bigger truck. He found an older Ford F-250 that was perfect. He put a down payment on it and was set to grow with his business. The truck was a four-wheel-drive model and would carry more than his old Toyota that the boy had sold for more than he paid for it...after driving it for four years.

About four days after his purchase, he pulled onto the freeway and brought his new truck up to highway speed. Then it happened: a clunk from the transmission. The boy took it to a transmission place. They took it for a test drive. The boy waited patiently, and the man behind the counter said the guy who was test driving never had taken this long before. *Why did he have to say that?* the boy thought to himself.

Finally he came back, sat down at a desk, and started adding on an old adding machine. Every time he entered more numbers, the boy cringed. Now the mechanic was done. "Five thousand, eight hundred dollars," he said, but that included six recalls on that transmission that had not been done.

The boy just looked at him, searching for something to say. "Can I have a copy of that?" he finally blurted out. "Sure," the guy said.

The boy was going back to the dealership where he had bought the truck. Reaching his destination, he looked for the salesman that had sold it to him. There he was going into the showroom. He soon caught up with him and showed him the quote. The salesman looked at it and said matter-of-factly, "Sorry, you've had the vehicle for over three days, so there's nothing we can do for you."

Dejected, the boy just looked at him. *I don't have $5,800,* he thought to himself as he walked back to his truck.

The next day the boy took it to the Ford dealership near his apartment. He explained the situation to the service lady who met him, and she said they would do a brand-new repair quote for him. The boy thanked her and sat down in the waiting lounge. Had God really directed me to this truck? Why would he do this? Was there some sort of lesson to be learned here? The boy was confused. He put his head in his hands. The business would not go on. He would have to buy a piece of junk cheap, a real cheap piece of junk to drive. He would be fixing it left and right. It was going to be...oh no, the service lady was back.

She looked at him slowly rising out of his seat. His face must have said it all because she said, "Looks like you just lost your best friend."

"Well I was directed to that truck and now look where I am," the boy replied.

"Well let me give you the quote," she said. "It comes to $6,900 total," she said. "But whoever directed you to this truck was pretty smart," she said to him. The boy was dumbstruck. *What is she talking about? It's $6,900!* She smiled and continued. "Seems there was a five-year transferable warranty purchased on the drive train, so after the deductible, Ford will pay for the rest."

The boy couldn't believe it! He asked quickly, "How much is the deductible"? She said, "Fifty dollars." He said simply, with tears rising in his eyes, "Go ahead and fix it."

The Lord had done this. It was his wisdom, but it was disguised. It required something, and that was "faith." Not a little faith, but a big faith, and the boy had not done too well on God's test.

> *2 Chronicles 20:20 "Have faith in the Lord your God and you will be upheld."*
>
> *Habakkuk 2:4 "But the righteous will live by His faith."*
>
> *Romans 3:22 "This righteousness from God comes through faith in Jesus Christ to all who believe."*
>
> *Romans 10:17 "Consequently, faith comes from hearing the message and the message is heard through the word of Christ."*

> *1 Corinthians 1:24 "Not that we Lord it over your faith, but we work with you for your joy, because it is by faith you stand firm."*
>
> *James 2:22 "You see that His faith and His actions were working together, and His faith was made complete by what he did."*
>
> *1 Peter 1:21 "Through Him, you believe in God, who raised Him from the dead and glorified Him and so your faith and hope are in God."*

Now the boy was continuing to build his business when one morning he watched airplanes flying into buildings in New York. A most horrific tragedy that shocked the nation. An attack on the United States soil, affecting many people and having ripple effects everywhere.

The boy was used to the phone ringing often. He was up early to make sure he answered every call personally. Suddenly the phone stopped ringing — not all together, but gradually the calls became less and less. How did something three thousand miles away affect his business? People were in shock, but in addition, they were scared. Business ground down to a trickle of what it was before.

The boy wasn't able to meet his debt obligations. Things were going downhill. He had to do something. He went for legal advice. The advice: file bankruptcy. The boy wanted to see where God was in all of this, but he was not getting any directional ideas.

One day the pastor in charge of seniors said he had a project for him: people living close to the church and in need of Bible study. The boy took the project on. He called the people and set up a time for Bible study. The boy, eager to make a good impression and get started, arrived early. Only one woman was there. Her husband and the other couple were across the hall in another apartment. In order for them to bolster themselves for Bible study, they were drinking beer and doing drugs.

So the boy tried to get as much information from the one person he was faced with at the time. It happened that her husband used to be a mechanic and had gotten laid off. He had had a tough life. At eighteen he walked into a room where his father was just as he pulled the trigger to the rifle in his mouth. He and his wife had used heroin on and off. They also had a small child. The woman swore she had stopped heroin and that the other three were the ones who needed help.

The boy did his best to talk to them, but their own stories were better, so he used them. Seems the couple across the hall had lived in Washington in a mobile home. One late afternoon, it had caught fire and burned to the bare frame. The fireman said it was a total loss and only one thing escaped the blaze. He reached into his coat pocket and produced a Bible, totally untouched by the fire. Everything by it had burned to ashes. The boy asked if they could see any significance in the Bible not being torched. The boy told them it was from God himself trying to give them a message.

The boy continued to try to do Bible study each week, but after several weeks, the people would cancel for some insignificant reason. The one couple's car had bald rear tires, so the boy showed up at the wife's work with two used tires that he had gotten for them. She said, "Thank you," and went back to work. The boy brought them a dresser and some other things, but no change occurred.

One day he got a call from the church. A hysterical woman was at the hospital requesting the boy. So he immediately grabbed his Bible and headed to the hospital. It was the couple from across the hall. Her husband, about forty years old, was in serious trouble. His wife met the boy crying and being hysterical. She was screaming for help.

The boy talked to the ICU nurse. She informed him that her husband was A, B, C positive for hepatitis. An infectious bacteria was in his bloodstream, and he had about ten hours to live. He said he was with the church and that he would like to pray over the man. She reluctantly said yes. His wife wanted to come in also, but the nurse said no.

When the nurse brought him into the room, the man was tilted with his head lower than his feet. The nurse said it was to keep his blood in the brain. The boy put his Bible in his hand and prayed over the man. Then he returned to the waiting area, where the wife was located. She was beside herself, and he talked to her and listened to her and provided comfort in the best way he could. The boy then left, and nine hours later the man's wife called him and said that he had died. The boy was in shock for a couple of days.

Then the senior pastor called him. He had a thirty-year-old man who was an alcoholic and had been in and out of rehab facilities and hospitals. The boy went to see him. He did not have a good feeling about this because of his own history.

His name was Doug, and he was a worship leader. He played the guitar in a small church in eastern Oregon. He had a job and wanted the boy to drive him to work so he wouldn't have to ride his bike. The boy asked him if he was going to the boy's church, and he said yes. The boy didn't have work to do, so he took him to the Goodwill to buy him shirts, ties, and a couple of sports coats.

So the boy picked him up for church and went to see him often. One day he arrived at Doug's apartment, and Doug was really mad. The boy asked him what was wrong. Doug said his vacuum cleaner had died, and he wanted a new one, one without any bags. The boy said, "Do you have money"? He said, "No." The boy stayed for dinner. Doug loved to barbecue, and he was making teriyaki chicken on a small BBQ that looked really old. Doug said while cooking that the teriyaki sauce he had was no good and he really would like some of the thick, gourmet sauces that were available. The boy tried to say it was good enough, whatever he was using, and they ate their meal talking and laughing.

The next day, a professional lady wanted a quick haul away of some stuff in her garage. Her mother was flying the next day, so it all had to go fast. The boy arrived early, and as was his custom, he separated items into the truck by recycling area they would go to in his small storage facility: cardboard, thrift shop, wood, etc. So as he was going through one box, he felt a glass bottle, but it was full. The lady was a drinker, so he wanted to check the bottle quickly while she was upstairs getting more stuff. He pulled the bottle out and looked at the label: premium teriyaki thick BBQ sauce. The boy just looked at it in amazement. He walked to the cab of the truck and threw it in the seat.

Finally he was loaded, and he gave the woman the price. Then she said, "Oh I have one more item." The boy said he would wait, and she returned with a brand-new bagless canister vacuum and said, "I have to get rid of this because it's too heavy for me to use." The boy said, "Are you sure?" She said, "Yes, I've already bought a much lighter one."

The boy, amazed again, put it in the front seat of the truck. He went to call Doug to see if he needed a ride, but he was already home. The boy said, "Wait till you see what I have for you." Doug asked, "What is it?" The boy said, "I'm on my way over."

The boy carried both items up the stairs and knocked on the door. Doug came to the door and couldn't believe his eyes. "Isn't this what you asked for?" the boy said. Doug just nodded and gave him a big hug.

Two nights later while having BBQ again, Doug was having problems with his BBQ and asked if he ever ran across BBQs in his work. The boy said they were far and few at that and usually beat up or broken.

So the next day, the boy had a carpet job to do. He did the removal, and after he was loaded and ready to go, the lady said, "Can you take one more thing for me?" The boy said, "Sure, no problem." She pointed him to a thirty-six-inch gas BBQ with a side burner and extra propane tank and an all-weather cover for the unit. The boy was in amazement again. Praise the Lord!

The boy called Doug and said he had another surprise for him. Doug wanted to know so bad. He asked for just a hint at what it was. The boy said, "I'm on the way." The boy knocked on the apartment door and said, "I can't even carry this one up to your apartment."

Doug went flying down the stairs to the boy's truck. He was so excited when he saw it, he could barely contain himself. They struggled to get the BBQ up the stairs to Doug's apartment deck. Doug said, "Let's have dinner!" The boy agreed.

Now a couple of weeks passed, and Doug called and said he was in trouble. The boy asked, "What's the problem?" Doug didn't want to say. Grudgingly Doug said he had spent his whole paycheck getting drunk over the weekend and needed to go to the detox center at a hospital across town. The boy cleared his schedule and drove him to the hospital. Doug said it would probably be two or three days until he was out. He wanted the boy to clean up his apartment because it was cluttered with beer cans and bottles. The boy said, "No problem. I'll take care of it."

The boy went back to the apartment and found over fifty cans and bottles. Mostly they were the largest size. The boy filled two plastic trash bags and straightened up the living room and kitchen. Then he left for the grocery store. He recycled all the cans and bottles. It came to over fifteen dollars, so the boy bought two thick, premium steaks and put them in Doug's refrigerator.

A couple days later at Bible study, the boy told about the miraculous signs and wonders he found for Doug. He also told them about Doug's weekend. A few said he should give up on Doug, like everyone else had, even his relatives and old church congregation.

The boy answered them. "The Lord never gave up on me. He consistently stayed with me for over forty years until I finally came around to Jesus!" They told him he was crazy.

A few weeks later while having dinner at Doug's, the boy learned there was a Promise Keepers event coming soon. Doug had invited two friends from his old church to go with him, but he needed a mattress or something to sleep on because they were driving from eastern Oregon. Doug said a hide-a-bed would be what he would like because he had no couch in his living room. The boy explained that he had picked up a lot of hide-a-beds from rentals that people left, but they were either broken or really soiled.

The boy was looking for another miraculous sign by the Lord, but after a few days, nothing happened. Then an old customer said he had three rolls of carpet to haul away at one of his rental houses. Could the boy show up the next day in the morning? The boy said, "Sure, I'll be there."

The boy showed up, and the customer opened the garage door. There lay the three rolls of carpet. The boy loaded them up and gave the customer the price. The customer said, "Could you take one more thing?" "Yes," the boy replied. "What is it?" The customer walked to the back of the garage, grabbed a tarp, and pulled it off a brand-new hide-a-bed. The customer opened it up, and the mattress was still in a plastic bag. They loaded it up.

The boy called Doug and said, "You better find two more guys because I've got something for you!"

Doug could not believe it. He was in the parking lot of the apartments when the boy drove up. The boy had a tarp over it, tied down by ropes. He untied the ropes, took the tarp off, and Doug was in shock. "Wow, it looks good," Doug said.

The boy said, "It's almost brand-new!" Doug was overcome with joy. It took four people twenty minutes to maneuver the stairs and get it in Doug's apartment. The boy talked to Doug about God's favor being on him and how this was a sign to stop drinking. Doug, more or less, acknowledged that fact, but a few weeks later they were driving to the hospital detox center again.

Acts 2:43 "Everyone was filled with awe and many wonders and miraculous signs were done."

Psalms 77:14 "You are the God who performs miracles."

Job 5:9 "He performs wonders that cannot be fathomed, miracles that cannot be counted."

This time a mandatory AA meeting was required and weekly urinalysis also. The boy took him to all the meetings and picked him up also.

Doug called the boy and said, "Please come to dinner." The boy was eager to help Doug celebrate eight weeks of the program. Doug said he had to talk to the boy about something. The boy listened intently as Doug described the way he had been drinking and beating the urinalysis tests.

The boy was heartbroken but told Doug he forgave him. The boy wanted to know what's next. He said, "A picnic by the river at an amusement park." Doug said he wanted a girlfriend, and sure enough he met a Christian girl at the picnic. A big romance ensued over a number of months.

Then one day the boy, Doug, and his girlfriend were out for a meal. Doug said, "We are thinking about getting married!" The boy said, "That's great. Just make sure you wait about six months to a year." "Why?" they asked. The boy said, "You have not known each other long enough." The boy looked for their reactions.

Later he took Doug's girlfriend aside and told her about all the relapses Doug had over the years so she could think logically about what she was getting into in this marriage. But after a couple of months, they had set a date, and the boy was going to be the best man. So they got married, although a big traffic nightmare on the freeway almost spoiled the event. But the justice of the peace and all the guests waited patiently even after the appointed hour.

Three months later, Doug relapsed again, and his wife was calling the boy. This time the boy found twenty-five whipped cream cans in the back of Doug's truck. Inhaling the gas was a shortcut high. But Doug had a high tolerance because of his history with alcohol.

Doug soon had to move in with the boy. He had a two-bedroom apartment, and the boy could take him to church. This only lasted awhile, and then Doug's parents in eastern Oregon were going to let him live with them. The boy talked to his aunt at length, but she said no. His cousin, a nurse, said no also.

Doug asked the boy as they were going to the storage facility to get his stuff, "What kind of a Christian are you, anyway?" The boy was confused and said, "What do you mean?" Doug answered, "Everyone has given up on me, but you came every time I called, no matter what the circumstances. Tell me why."

"Read the Bible, Doug. It's all in there." Doug died at the age of thirty-two of a bacterial infection that got into his blood. No alcohol or drugs were found during the autopsy.

> *Mark 12:28 "'Of all the commandments which is the most important?' 'The most important one,' Jesus answered, 'is this. Hear O Israel, the Lord our God, the Lord is one. Love the Lord, your God with all your heart and with all your soul and with all your mind and with all your strength. The second is this: Love your neighbor as yourself. There is no commandment greater than these.'"*

So for the boy's next big mistake, he decided to move to Phoenix, where his sister lived and the housing boom was in full swing. To this day, it was the biggest blunder he would make and would permanently kill his business for good.

> *Proverbs 19:21 "Many are the plans in a man's heart, but it is the Lord's purpose that prevails."*

> *Proverbs 15:22 "Plans fail for lack of counsel."*

> *Proverbs 16:3 "Commit to the Lord whatever you do and your plans will succeed."*

> *Isaiah 30:1 "'Woe to the obstinate children,' declares the Lord, 'to those who carry out plans that are not mine.'"*

Although the boy tried hard to make a new start in Arizona, his networking and sales calls yielded very little business. Six months later, he got up one morning to go to his truck in his apartment complex, and it was gone. Arizona has one of the highest car-theft and truck-theft rates in the nation. All his paperwork, his tools, and office files were gone. The truck was stolen by coyotes, those who smuggle Hispanics across the border.

The boy was deflated by the situation and thought about returning home to Oregon, but he found a job selling home security systems. Soon he rose to be the top salesman and tried to save money to return to Oregon. He bought an old Oldsmobile and paid cash from the settlement on his truck because it could not be repaired.

Now he met a person who told him about a large church in Mesa, Arizona. He began attending regularly. He tried to get into teaching Bible study, but there were no positions available. The boy loved going to the church, for it was doing unconventional preaching, which attracted interest in the community. For example, one Sunday morning there was a bass boat on the stage. Another Sunday the preacher rode his Harley Davidson down the aisle to the stage. It was unconventional, but it filled the church with thousands of people.

The boy received a business offer from a man in Oregon he knew. So he started the process of finding a moving company. The boy made sure his top picks had been in business several years, were listed with the Better Business Bureau, and belonged to the moving and storage association. The boy packed all the boxes by himself and sold or gave away some of the furniture. Then the day arrived for the move. His new apartment complex in Oregon required renter's insurance, so he had purchased it three days before the move.

His car packed with items he would need on the three-day drive to Oregon, he said good-bye to his sister and headed back to Oregon. His trip was uneventful and passed quickly. Once he arrived in Oregon, he moved in, sleeping on an air bed he had purchased. He called the movers, but there was a delay, and it lasted three weeks.

Chapter Six

The movers called him finally and said there had been an accident in Idaho with the moving truck. A week later, he went to a warehouse in Oregon to inspect what he was about to receive. At least 65 percent of his possessions were gone. He had some dishes, two boxes of clothes, a desk, and his bed. Various other items were in boxes, but he could not open those until he paid seven hundred dollars to the driver in cash when delivered. The boy quizzed the driver about what had happened in the accident. The driver said he was trying to avoid hitting a deer when he ran into a guardrail, which opened a big hole from the front to the back on the side of the trailer. Five families' possessions poured out on the road. A police officer ordered a front-end loader and dump trucks to haul everything on the road to the dump. The boy couldn't believe it!

He called his insurance company for advice on what to do. They told him that his renter's insurance covered it all, and they would send him some forms.

The only drawback was the insurance company required him to spend money and turn in receipts for reimbursement. So it was a long process, and he didn't have a lot of extra money. He was living paycheck to paycheck.

His new job was a night job delivering satchels of correspondence to banks, mortgage, realtor, and other professional offices. He had to drive his own car and pay for his own gas and other items the company provided.

One night he pulled to a signal to cross a four-lane road. He pressed down on the gas as the light turned green. The car would not move. It never had done this before. As the boy sat there for what seemed like minutes, a large truck coming from his left ran the red light. He was in shock. Then his car came to life and pulled across the street. Wow! Praise the Lord!

> *Job 12:10 "In His hand is the life of every creature, and the breath of all mankind."*
>
> *Psalm 25:20 "Guard my life and rescue me; let me not be put to shame, for I take refuge in You."*
>
> *Psalm 119:154 "Preserve my life according to your promise."*
>
> *Mathew 10:39 "Whoever finds his life will lose it, and whoever loses his life for My sake will find it."*
>
> *John 14:6 "I am the way and the truth and the life. No one comes to the Father except through Me."*

Another day the boy was sitting at a signal with a friend. "The light is green," the friend said. Just as the boy was to pull out, a semitruck doing about forty miles an hour with a large load of steel ran the red light. Now almost in the middle of the intersection, he looked straight at the semi's driver. He just smiled and waved, not touching his brakes.

The boy now looked for another job at another delivery company. He was soon hired and began work. The boy was working for a Middle Eastern man who had a big family.

This job was daily package delivery that involved many stops and packages. The day then came for his boss to sell his business. He sold not only his business, but sold the boy along with the business. The boy was now over sixty years old and could barely do the job each day. Some days were harder than others, but the boy pushed himself to complete his tasks each day. But he called frequently on the Lord to help him with his daily tasks, and the Lord answered his prayers.

Lessons Learned

1. I don't run from God!
As you can probably see now, I have spent many years trying to do what I wanted instead of what God wanted. I have made serious mistakes and sins throughout my life, but God was always there trying to direct my steps to come back to him. God is that way. His unconditional love is hard for us because we don't always recognize it in the world we live today.

Something else is always trying to get our attention, so we don't have to think about God and what he wants us to do for him. The electronic age — with cell phones, iPods, iPads, wireless computers, and laptops, et al. — requires us to commit more and more time to texting, Twitter, Facebook, and just browsing the Internet.

I seriously believe everyone who is committing time to physical fitness and media needs to stop for one hour a day to work on their spiritual sides.

God is pretty much a done deal with over 90 percent of Americans believing there is a God, so if you are in the 10 percent minority, why? But do you have a relationship with him?!

God has already completed all the work justifying the entire human race to himself. That's what Jesus did on the cross, reconciling all of us to God. So the work is done. All you have to do is accept the free invitation from God through Jesus his son.

2. Faith is belief in Jesus!

> *Mathew 6:40 "For my Father's will is that everyone who looks to the Son and believes in him shall have eternal life and I will raise him up at the last day."*
>
> *Mathew 5:24 "I tell you the truth, whoever hears My word and believes in Him who sent me has eternal life and will not be condemned; he has crossed over from death to life."*

The question has always been, "What are you going to do with Jesus?" There are only two choices: reject him or accept him. There is no middle ground. It's not a choice that someone else can make for himself or herself. It's totally up to you.

If you are wrong, consider this: All of us are searching for something. After years of asking questions, there's just two answers: I want to find a true love of my life or I want to live forever. Well God has given us a spirit that cannot be snuffed out by physical death. It's going to live for eternity. And your choices are two: It's heaven or hell! So, okay, what about hell? See what Jesus says:

Luke 16:19-31 "There was a rich man who was dressed in purple and fine linen and lived in luxury every day. At his gate, lay a beggar named Lazarus, covered with sores and longing to eat what fell from the rich man's table. Even the dogs came and licked his sores. The time came when the beggar died and the angels carried him to Abraham's side. The rich man also died and was buried. In Hell, where he was in torment, he looked up and saw Abraham far away with Lazarus by his side. So he called to him, 'Father Abraham, have pity on me and send Lazarus to dip the tip of his finger in water and cool my tongue, because I am in agony in this fire.' But Abraham replied, 'Son remember that in your lifetime, you received good things while Lazarus received bad things, but now he is comforted here and you are in agony. And besides all this, between us and you a great chasm has been fixed, so that those who want to go from here to you cannot nor can anyone cross over from there to us.' He answered, 'Then, I beg you, Father, send Lazarus to my father's house, for I have five brothers Let him warn them, so that they will not also come to this place of torment.' Abraham replied, 'They have Moses and the Prophets; let them listen to them.' 'No, Father Abraham,' he said, 'but if someone from the dead goes to them, they will repent.' He said to him, 'If they do not listen to Moses and the Prophets, they will not be convinced even if someone rises from the dead.'"

We should take note of several things in Jesus' parable:

The rich man lived in luxury every day.

The rich man is fully conscious in hell.

The rich man feels the heat: "I am in agony in this fire."

Between heaven and hell is a separation that cannot be crossed.

The rich man wants to save his five brothers from what he calls "a place of torment."

Abraham refers to the Old Testament, which refers consistently to Jesus.

Isaiah 53:1-7 "Who has believed our message and to whom has the arm of the Lord been revealed? He grew up before him like a tender shoot, he had no beauty or majesty to attract us to Him, nothing in his appearance that we should desire him. He was despised and rejected by men. A man of sorrows, and familiar with suffering. Like one from whom men hide their faces. He was despised, we esteemed him not. Surely he took up our infirmities and carried our sorrows, yet we considered him stricken by God smitten by him and afflicted. But he was pierced for our transgressions, he was crushed for our iniquities, the punishment that brought us peace was upon Him, and by His wounds we are healed. We all like sheep have gone astray, each of us has turned to his own way; and the Lord has laid on him the iniquity of us all. He was oppressed and afflicted, yet He did not open His mouth; He was led like a lamb to the slaughter, and as a sheep before her shearers is silent, so He did not open His mouth."

Isaiah 52:13-15 "See my servant will act wisely; he will be raised and lifted up and highly exalted. Just as there were many who were appalled at him, his appearance, so disfigured beyond that of any man. And his form marred beyond human likeness, so he will sprinkle many nations and kings will shut their mouths because of him. For what they were not told, they will see, and what they have not heard, they will understand."

Isaiah wrote these words estimated at 740 to 680 B.C., seven hundred years before Jesus was born. How does Isaiah do this? It is a revelation from God, just like Jesus' birth.

Isaiah 7:14 "Therefore the Lord himself will give you a sign; the virgin will be with child and will give birth to a son and will call him Immanuel (which means God with us)."

3. Be born again, repent, turn around, go another way, don't continue on the path to hell!

> *John 3:3-8 "In reply Jesus declared, 'I tell you the truth, no one can see the kingdom of God unless he is born again.' 'How can a man be born when he is old,' Nicodemus asked. 'Surely he can not enter a second time into his mother's womb to be born.' Jesus answered, 'I tell you the truth, no one can enter the kingdom of God unless he is born of water and spirit. Flesh gives birth to flesh, but the spirit gives birth to spirit. You should not be surprised at my saying, you must be born again. The wind blows wherever it pleases. You hear its sound, but you can not tell where it comes from or where it is going. So it is with everyone born of the spirit.'"*

> *John 10:9 "I am the gate, whoever enters through me will be saved."*

> *Matthew 7:13-14 "Enter through the narrow gate. For wide is the gate and broad is the road that leads to destruction and many enter through it. But small is the gate and narrow the road that leads to life, and only a few find it."*

> *1 John 5:1 "Everyone who believes that Jesus is the Christ is born of God and everyone who loves the Father, loves his child as well."*

> *John 6:29 "Then they asked him, 'What must we do to do the works of God?' Jesus answered, 'The work of God is this; to believe in the one he has sent.'"*

So scriptures say it over and over: Being born of God is through Jesus. There is no other way.

> *John 14:6 "I am the way and the truth and the life. No one comes to the Father except through me."*

Chapter 6½

Faith...

On January 12, 2012, one day past my birthday, at age sixty-four, I fell and hurt my right, inside calf on my leg while working for a major package express company.

I worked the day and finished in the afternoon because the skin was not broken, and it just looked like a scrape. I showed up for work on January 13 and worked six hours delivering packages, but my leg was now purple and red from just below the knee all the way to the ankle. The entire area was starting to swell and starting to hurt very badly.

I had insurance via my military service, so I went to the local clinic to have them look at the wound. They had two doctors look at the wound, consulted, and said I needed to go to the emergency room at the local hospital. I was still in my delivery uniform, so I showed the receiving nurse my leg, and she said someone would be right with me. I knew what that meant: hurry up and wait!

Finally I was put in an exam room, triaged, and told to wait for a doctor. Over the next four hours, I was seen by three doctors, each with a bit more experience than the previous one. The third doctor was concerned because I was taking Cumadin, a blood thinner. He said I might be bleeding inside my leg from a broken blood vessel. I said my doctor was Jesus. He dismissed it politely.

He said a CT scan would reveal if I was bleeding, so I was soon heading upstairs to the CT scanning department. The CT scan showed I was bleeding from a broken blood vessel in my leg. It was filling the space between the skin and the muscle.

By 12:30 A.M. the next morning, I was being admitted to the hospital and had a NBM order placed on me (nothing by mouth). No water, no food, no medication, nothing!

Soon the vascular surgical team came to see me — about four people. They said a large blood clot was forming in my leg, and I may need surgery to remove it. I asked about the NBM order. They said it was in preparation for surgery.

Saturday afternoon I was tired from no sleep because of vitals check every two hours, blood draws two times a day, and various people coming and going.

A conclusion by the vascular surgical team was reached. I was a high-risk surgery patient. They had decided to transfuse me with a plasma product to counteract the blood thinner's effect. This would allow my body's defense system to heal the broken blood vessel. As if by magic, it would all be fixed. However, my leg continued to swell.

I was feeling better — might have been the pain meds, but I was telling jokes and saying my trust was in the Lord! After transfusing me, they cancelled the NBM order, and I could have food.

Soon the vascular team was back, concerned about my blood pressure being so high at 157 over 110! I simply said, "Well I haven't had my blood pressure meds for two days so...." They replied that was probably the reason! Glad I had not changed my routine. I was reading my Bible twice a day and praying in thanksgiving and praise to the Lord.

By Saturday night, the vascular team said everything looked good for me to be discharged Sunday afternoon. At 1:30 P.M., I was discharged. They said to change the bandage daily and keep it wrapped tightly with an Ace bandage, so I left feeling somewhat happy. I think it was because I was leaving the hospital.

Everything was going great until I called my primary care physician and talked to the nurse, who put me on hold three times trying to figure out why I was calling. She told me I didn't need to see the doctor. "Just keep doing what you're doing," she said, and go to the physical-therapy appointment in two weeks. This would mean since my hospital visit, I would have not seen a medical person for thirty days.

So two weeks later, I went to the physical-therapy appointment. I was now aligned with my employer's workers' comp insurer receiving weekly disability checks. It was March 1. The wound had changed dramatically. I was changing the bandage two to three times a day.

The physical-therapy nurse looked at the wound unwrapped and immediately left the room for the physical therapist. He took one look at the wound and said, "It smells bad. It is infected, and your skin is rotting away. You need to see your primary care doctor." He gave me a cane to walk with and said to try to keep off my right leg.

I called the doctor and got the nurse, and she said the first available appointment was March 7 — a week away. No choice, so I set the appointment.

The wound continued to pour out a bloody, watery type of liquid. By the time the time rolled around for the appointment, I was still changing the bandages three times a day. At the doctor's office, the bandage was soaked clear through to the jeans I was wearing. The nurse freaked out. The doctor said I needed to go to the emergency room again.

Now the workers' comp insurer has told me a couple weeks earlier that with any changes in my condition, I was to call them immediately. So I called and told them the situation. They said my current health provider was done due to mismanagement of the situation. She said to pick any private hospital, and they would call ahead and let them know they were in charge now. They would give them all the billing information, so I didn't have to worry about anything.

Totally different emergency room — I was seen almost immediately, and I had five doctors surrounding me and listening to my story of what had happened since January. Most said my wound was really impressive. I said my trust was in the Lord. I was also telling jokes to make everyone smile!

Soon I was admitted and went to the eighth floor to a private room. Almost instantly antibiotic fluids were hanging on my IV pole.

Soon I found out my surgeon would be the head of the surgical department, who sat as chairman of the hospital's quality committee. Two or three of my nurses were also Christians.

The Lord said;
Exodus 23:30 "Little by little, I will drive them out before you, until you have increased enough to take possession of the land."

Exodus 33:2 "I will send an angel before you and drive out the Canaanites, Amorites, Hittites, Perizzites, Hivites and Jebusites."

Deut 1:30 "The Lord your God, who is going before you will fight for you as he did in Egypt, before your very eyes and in the desert."

Deut 31:8 "The Lord himself goes before you and will be with you; He will never leave you or forsake you. Do not be afraid; do not be discouraged."

The Lord had gone before me and prepared everything ahead of time, increasing my faith and trust in Him!

At various times, someone was taking my vital signs, giving me meds, or changing my IV bag. But the weird thing was the "vampire nurse"; she came every night between 2:30 and 3:00 A.M. Result: no sleep, except in three- or four-hour periods if no one else came into the room.

I was put on a protein diet and ordered my meals from an extensive menu. I would call, and about thirty minutes later it would show up. It was like a hotel with room service.

Soon I was scheduled for surgery, and I was amazingly calm. I felt the Lord's presence and remembered the word: "I will always be with you." Someone showed up to take me to pre-op. I was feeling great because it was finally happening, and the Lord Jesus had gone before me, selecting each person to fulfill his will and purpose for me.

While I was testifying to this fact to the nurses in pre-op, one of them leaned over and whispered, "No worries, your golden." Surgery lasted ninety minutes. The only strange thing was the operating room was really cold temperature wise.

In post-op I woke up with nurses asking me how I was feeling. I said I was fine, and they gave me some crushed ice to suck on frequently. The hole in my leg was 6 inches long, 2½ inches wide, and 2 inches deep.

Back up in my room, a group of nurses showed up in some sort of training session. They were there to install a wound vacuum on my leg, which would allow it to heal three or four times faster.

Of course they placed the wound-vac on the IV pole, so I was tethered like a dog on a chain. Obviously this made bathing, restroom visits, and eating a little more difficult.

The head doctor showed up in my room. This was like the hospital's troubleshooter or patient's advocate. He asked how I was feeling and then said he had to disclose something to me because it was required. Oh boy, what now?

He said the IV of antibiotics prior to surgery was in essence a plan to get my blood level to 25 percent antibiotics. He said they were a little overzealous in this area and went beyond the 25 percent level. He then said my kidneys had taken a hit. So what does that mean? He couldn't tell me, but it wasn't good.

I gave this little bump in the road to the Lord. I asked when I was going to be discharged. He said in a couple of days.

The next day my surgeon showed up, looked at the wound, and poked and prodded me. He looked like he was searching, but he didn't say anything. Finally he called the nurse in and told her to order an ultrasound on my leg. She asked why. He said he was expecting a DVT. Then he left. So I called my sister in Phoenix and asked her what it was. She told me it was really serious. They were looking for a blood clot in one of my main arteries. She said it could go to my brain or heart and I would die. I gave that to the Lord also. The result of the ultrasound: negative for a DVT.

A couple days later, the head doctor guy showed up again. I asked when I was going to be discharged. He said again "a couple of days." I said I was frustrated by all the interruptions to my sleep. He said this was normal and I just had to live with the inconvenience. I asked him if a person slept seven to eight hours a night, just had surgery, and was now not sleeping more than twelve to fifteen hours a week, what would he recommend for him to heal better? More sleep or the same twelve to fifteen hours a week. He thought about it and said he would push to get me discharged the next day.

Upon discharge they told me I would have to have do daily bandage changes with the wound-vac for the first five or so weeks. A nursing service was set up for daily visits.

Next I found out my employer had replaced me, so I called workers' comp to ask if he was required by law to hold my job. They said no. An Oregon law had been passed allowing employers with twenty or fewer employees to replace employees on workers' comp. Great.

Now I was receiving permanent disability income from my boss's workers' comp insurer: 66⅔ of my weekly pay.

My boss had cut my wages in half, so I had to take my Social Security early. My boss paid on Medicare and Social Security taxes, but no state or federal tax was deducted from my check. I found this out upon receiving my W-2 since I hadn't received a check stub, which was against the law. The end result: I owed the federal government and the state thousands of dollars.

Six months after my injury, I was released to return to work by my doctor. Workers' comp checks stopped, and I went on unemployment. I was still reading my Bible and praying twice a day in thanksgiving and praise to Jesus, my God, my Savior, my friend, and ultimately my everything!

Sustainability is a word we hear more and more each day. But what does it mean? No depletion of a natural resource. Endurance or persevering in a manner so you don't use up your resource.

Faith is not something you sit on. Faith, faithful, or faithfully is used over 350 times in the Bible. So if the word of God considers it important, shouldn't we also?

Romans 5:1 "Since we have been justified by faith."

How?

Romans 3:25 "Faith in his blood."

2 Corinthians 10:15b "Our hope is that, as your faith continues to grow. Our area of activity among you will greatly expand."

So our faith grows and helps the Gospel be spread in an ever-widening area.

2 Corinthians 10:16 "So that we can preach the Gospel in regions beyond you."

Romans 4:20-21 "Yet he (Abraham) did not waiver through unbelief regarding the promise of God, but was strengthened in his faith and gave glory to God, being fully persuaded that God had power to do what he had promised."

2 Corinthians 1:24 "Because it is by faith you stand firm."

Abraham accepted God's word as true and complete. Why? Because God knows all; He is the beginning and the end. Like Abraham we must strengthen our faith but also the faith of others.

In the hospital, two nurses came into my room and caught me reading my Bible. One told me she was a new Christian and introduced me to her friend, another nurse. I asked her if she read her Bible regularly. She kind of stumbled in her reply but did say she had two Bibles, two different versions. She said she had read one of them all the way through and it took forever. So I asked her how many times she had done that. She said once and asked, "How many times have you read yours?" I said, "In seventeen years, somewhere between thirty-five or forty times." "Why did you do that"? she asked. I then showed her the flyleaf pages in front and back and all the things I had written down, with page numbers or chapter and verse. She was amazed and copied some of them down. "You know the more you read, the more you grow, and you will always discover something new," I replied. Suddenly they were both very interested, and I gave them my three-stage plan to read Genesis to Maps in three months, six months or twelve months.

> *Romans 10:17 "Consequently, faith comes from hearing the message, and the message is heard through the word of Christ."*

Suddenly the nurses said, "Wow, we have to go." I told them to get a concordance and a bible commentary or two written by a group of scholars, not just one person. I told them this would help them if they were struggling with a particular passage or verse.

> *Romans 14a: "Accept him whose faith is weak without passing judgment."*
>
> *Romans 15:1 "We who are strong ought to bear with the failings of the weak and not to please ourselves."*
>
> *Colossians 2:6-7 "So then, just as you received Christ Jesus as Lord, continue to live in Him, rooted and built up in Him, strengthened in the faith as you were taught, and over flowing with thankfulness."* (Please note, "live in Him and "built up in Him." This shows us it is a process of walking in our new life in Christ. What is the result? "Strengthened in the faith." Can we really say we have enough faith? Seriously, you don't need more?)
>
> *1 Thessalonians 3:10 "Night and day we pray most earnestly that we may see you again and supply what is lacking in your faith."*
>
> *Jude 1:20 "But you dear friend, build yourselves up in your most holy faith and pray in the Holy Spirit."*

Faith is imparted to us by Jesus with our belief in who he is, that being God. If you believe you are full up with faith, you need to read the word more and more.

Continuing to work on our reading and study of God's word, we will build up our faith, by Christ's power and His desire to complete the good work starting in us.

> *Philippians 1:6b "Being confident of this, that he who began a good work in you will carry it on to completion until the day of Christ Jesus."*

Chapter Eight

4. Love one another.

> *John 15:9 Jesus said "as the Father has loved me, so I have loved you. Now remain in my love. If you obey my commands, you will remain in my love, just as I have obeyed my Father's commands and remain in his love. I have told you this so that my joy may be in you and that your joy may be complete. My command is this: Love each other as I have loved you. Greater love has no one than this, that he lay down his life for his friends! You are my friends if you do what I command."*

> *John 13:34-35 "A new command I give you: Love one another. As I have loved you, so you must love one another. By this all men will know that you are my disciples, if you love one another."*

Now to love someone you don't know too well or you maybe can't stand takes strength and commitment. If you really love someone, you will put it into action. Love is not a feeling; it's an action that you can see.

> *1 John 3:18 "Dear children, let us not love with words or tongue but with actions and truth."*

> *1 Cor 13:4-7 "Love is patient, love is kind. It does not envy, it does*

> *not boast, it is not proud. It is not rude, it is not self seeking, it is not easily angered, it keeps no record of wrongs. Love does not delight in evil but rejoices with truth. It always protects, always trusts, always hopes, always perseveres."*

> *1 Cor 13:13 "And now these three remain faith, hope and love. But the greatest of these is love."*

5. God has a plan for your life!

> *Ephesians 1:4-6 "For He chose us in Him before the creation of the world to be holy and blameless in His sight. In love, He predestined us to be adopted as His sons through Jesus Christ, in accordance with His pleasure and will — to the praise of His glorious grace, which He has freely given us in the ONE He loves."*

This is tough to wrap your mind around when we start talking before the creation of the world. But what does He say three times in Revelation 1:8, 21:6, *and* 22:13?

"I am the alpha and omega, the first and last, the beginning and the end."

He knows the past, present, and future of everything and everyone. So why do you look to others or yourself for an answer when God knows it all?

> *Philippians 1:6 Being confident of this that he who began a good work in you will carry it on to completion until the day of Christ Jesus."*

So you can see the action word here is began. He is waiting to start; the work is all done for you. Do you not want to be the best human being you can be?

> *Ephesians 1:11 "In Him we were also chosen, having been predestined according to the plan of Him who works out everything in conformity with the purpose of His will, in order that we, who were the first to hope in Christ might be for the praise of His glory."*

See there? "According to the plan" — does that not ripple with curiosity in your mind? What does the Creator of the universe and everything in it have planned for me?

Part of His plan is good works for us to do for others. If we love our neighbor, then we will help him or her to put our love into action.

> *Ephesians 2:10 "for we are God's workmanship, created in Christ Jesus to do good works, which God prepared in advance for us to do."*

The Lord has lots of things you can do for someone else, and get ready because it is more satisfying than you can believe. Remember, God's kingdom is upside down. The King didn't send us to die; he died for us, in our place.

Remember also God is justice supreme in all things, people, and ways.

> *Hebrews 6:10 "God is not unjust; He will not forget your work and the love you have shown Him as you have helped His people and continue to help them."*

> *Colossians 3:23-24 "Whatever you do, work at it with all your heart, as working for the Lord, not for men, since you know that you will receive an inheritance from the Lord as a reward. It is the Lord Christ you are serving."*

And what are you good at? Typing, filing, cheering up or…? Don't even think about it because when you come to Jesus, the Holy Spirit gives you a gift — yes really!

> *Ephesians 4:7-8 "But to each one of us grace has been given as Christ apportioned it. That's why it says: When He ascended on high, He led captives in His train and gave gifts to men."*

So some have this gift or that gift, but what matters is everyone has at least one. Greeter, usher, music, singer, teacher, or evangelist — all have a gift! Why?

> *Ephesians 4:12-13 "To prepare God's people for works of service, so that the body of Christ may be built up until we all reach unity*

> *in the faith and in the knowledge of the son of God and become mature, attaining to the whole measure of the fullness of Christ."*

In God's kingdom, everyone has the same value, so you are important to his plan.

6. What or who is the Holy Spirit?

> *Acts 2:38 "Peter replied, 'Repent and be baptized, every one of you, in the name of Jesus Christ for the forgiveness of sins and you will receive the gift of the Holy Spirit."*

The Holy spirit is unseen, but you can feel it and know its presence inside your body. He will help you make decisions, help you when you pray, and strengthen you against evil.

> *John 14: 15-17 "If you love me, you will obey what I command. And I will ask the Father and He will give you another counselor to be with you forever. The spirit of truth. The world can not accept Him, because it neither sees Him or knows Him, for He lives with you and will be in you."*

Are you excited yet? Not only do you get gifts, but you receive a helper to help you in all things, and he is with you forever — and much, much more.

Let's think about this. You are now overloaded with things, and now God gives you all this! Why do we need all that stuff? We just keep trying to find more room to put it all away. Look at the storage industry.

> *2 Corinthians 1:21-22 "Now it is God who makes both us and you stand firm in Christ. He anointed us, set his seal of ownership on us, and put his spirit in our hearts as a deposit, guaranteeing what is to come."*

7. How do we get to know God personally?

My Bible has study references, so a lot of pages are half pages or smaller. From Genesis to Revelation is 1,339 pages.

So let's say you want to read the Bible all the way through because it is God's word, no question about that, so what does that take?

1 year — 365 days x 4 pages a day = 1,460 pages (11½ months)

6 months — 180 days x 7.5 pages a day = 1,450 pages (6½ months)

4 months — 120 days x 11.2 pages a day = 1,344 pages (4 months)

Read your Bible twice a day or when you're searching for an answer or need help bad. It's truth — that's why so many people use it for life. It's the revealed word of God from way back (Dead Sea Scrolls, Moses).

We also get to know God because of the Holy Spirit. He reveals the spiritual things that a lot of people hear but don't understand.

> *1 Corinthians 2:8-10 "None of the rulers of this age understood it, for if they had, they would not have crucified the Lord of Glory. However, as it is written: (Isaiah 64:4) No eye has seen, no ear has heard, no mind has conceived what God has prepared for those that love him.*

But God has revealed it to us by His spirit.

> *1 Corinthian 2:11b "In the same way, no one knows the thoughts of God except the spirit of God."*

> *1 Corinthians 2:13 "This is what we speak, not in words taught us by human wisdom, but in words taught by the spirit, expressing spiritual truths in spiritual words."*

> *1 Corinthians 2:14 "The man without the spirit does not accept the things that come from the spirit of God, for they are foolishness to Him because they are spiritually discerned."*

I know what you are thinking: Why do these words over two thousand years old answer all the questions in our mind. Simple — God knew what questions all would have and supplied others to write them down for us. Is that cool or what?

To continue to understand God, stay in his Word, the Bible. By all means, don't just read it once. For as you continue in your reading, you will discover things you would claim you have never read before. After about twenty-five times, certain words stick in your mind, so a concordance (a list of words and where they are in the Bible) is a valuable tool. Soon also verses will be easier to remember. Verses spoken out loud during stressful times or while praying are very important. Because you're talking to God, He knows the verses also, but your ability to recall them identifies your commitment to God in your actions.

Remember, God likes to see us step out in faith by our actions, and then things start to happen!

8. God wants us to communicate with Him. Pray!

> *Deuteronomy 4:7 "What other nation is so great as to have their Gods near them the way the Lord our God is near us whenever we pray to Him?"*

> *Ephesians 6:18 "And pray in the spirit on all occasions with all kinds of prayers and requests."*

> *Philippians 4:6 "Do not be anxious about anything, but in prayer and petition, with thanksgiving present your request to God."*

A lot of people pray when things go wrong, there's a major crisis, during a disaster, or when they don't know where to turn! God is always listening. But if you pray consistently and regularly, you are in a special place with God, for so many don't do it consistently.

Jesus gave us directions that help us while praying.

> *Matthew 6:5-8 "And when you pray, do not be standing in the synagogues and on street corners to be seen by men. I tell you the truth, they have received their reward in full. But when you pray, go into your room, close the door and pray to your Father, who is unseen. Then your Father who sees what is done in secret, will reward you and when you pray, do not keep on babbling like the pagans, for they think they will be heard because of their many words. Do not be like them for your Father knows what you need before you ask Him."*

Some have never prayed before except maybe at meals or during some religious rituals. The good news is we have a helper to step in for us to get the right words to God even if we cannot compose in our minds what we need to say.

> *Romans: 8:26-27 "In the same way, the spirit helps us in our weakness. We do not know what we ought to pray for, but the spirit himself intercedes for us with groans that words can not express. And he who searches our hearts knows the mind of the spirit, because the spirit intercedes for the saints in accordance with God's will."*

> *Psalm 99:6b "They called on the Lord and he answered them."*

> *Isaiah 58:9a "Then you will call, and the Lord will answer; you will cry for help and He will say: 'Here am I.'"*

Do not forget you are talking to your creator, your savior, your God, but most importantly, your friend. He wants to do good for you and fill you with joy. Remember to show God reverence. Be in awe of Him and His mighty deeds done since the creation of the world. For He is truly your Father in heaven. Jesus said, "Which of you fathers, if your son asks for a fish, will give him a snake instead? Or if he asks for an egg, will give him a scorpion? If you then, though you are evil, know how to give good gifts to your children, how much more will your Father in heaven give the Holy Spirit to those that ask Him" (Luke 11:11).

Also, just because God knows what you need before you ask, be sure to ask anyway. You might say, "He knows what I'm thinking, so why do I have to ask?"

Jesus also said, "So I say to you, ask and it will be given to you; seek and you will find. Knock and the door will be opened to you. For everyone who asks receives; he who seeks finds; and to him who knocks the door will be opened" (Luke 11:9-10).

Chapter Nine

9. Tithes are a worship to God for what he has given you.
Less than 10 percent of churchgoing Christians tithe with a consistent weekly or monthly amount. Why? Because we are selfish basically and want to spend it on ourselves. Since God made everything, all that we have is His, and we are just stewards. You cannot take anything with you when you die. Someone else who didn't work for it gets it all.

> *Genesis 14:18 20 "Then Melchizedek King of Salem brought out bread and wine. He was priest of God most high and he blessed Abram saying, 'Blessed be Abram by God most high, creator of heaven and earth. And blessed be God most high who delivered your enemies into your hand.' Then Abram gave him a tenth of everything."*

How does God look at your tithe?

> *Leviticus 27:30 "A tithe of everything from the land, whether grain from the soil or fruit from the trees, belongs to the Lord, it is holy to the Lord."*

The Lord will definitely return the tithe multiplied so you will have more to tithe.

> *2 Corinthian 9:10-11 "Now he who supplies seed to sower and bread for food will also supply and increase your store of seed and will enlarge the harvest of your righteousness. You will be made rich in every way so that you can be generous on every occasion, and through us your generosity will result in thanksgiving to God."*

> *Malachi 3:10-11 "Bring the whole tithe into the storehouse, that there may be food in my house. 'Test me in this,' says the Lord almighty, 'and see if I will not throw open floodgates of heaven and pour out so much blessing that you will not have room enough for it.'"*

The Lord is our Father in heaven, and He is sovereign over all things and situations. Most people give something but not regularly and with a consistent amount. No other lesson has been clearly shown to me as tithing. Try it for two months, and you will be amazed at the results. You may even see a miracle happen.

Probably the best verse in the Bible as far as we live each day is this: "Remember this: whoever sows sparingly will also reap sparingly, and whoever sows generously will reap generously" (2 Corinthians 9:6).

This counts not only for tithing but for all we give out each day: smiles, laughter, hugs, encouragement, comfort, help, and, of course, love.

10. It's never too late or your condition too hopeless or too filled with sins and very bad choices.

> *2 Chronicles 30:9 "If you return to the Lord, then your brothers and your children will be shown compassion by their captors and will come back to this land, for the Lord your God is gracious and compassionate. He will not turn His face from you if you return to Him."*

> *Jeremiah 24:7 "I will give them a heart to know Me that I am the Lord. They will be my people, and I will be their God, for they will return to me with all their heart."*

> *Hosea 12:6 "But you must return to your God; maintain love and justice, and wait for your God always."*

> *Zechariah 1:3 "This is what the Lord almighty says: 'Return to me,' declares the Lord almighty, 'and I will return to you,' says the Lord almighty."*

Now you say you really messed up and you did all kinds of terrible things that you can't even bring yourself to talk about. The Lord already knows what has happened. You just need to confess it to Him and ask for His forgiveness. Well you may have heard of Goliath the giant and also about King David. He had an affair with a married woman whom he saw bathing from his palace roof. Her husband was at war for the king, and to cover up his sin, he had the man killed and took his wife as his own. Yes, that's adultery and murder.

Psalm 51 is David's plea to God to forgive him, and God did just that.

Read King David's story in 2 Samuel 11:1 to 12:23.

11. When God seems far away, you may feel all alone. What can you hold on to tightly?

Many Christians face this desperate situation, and it may last for awhile. Remember that God is all-seeing and ever-listening. Also, your prayers are not just hitting the ceiling and not going anywhere. God hears you. He is with you always. Grab for your hope first because hope of ours is unseen, and we know our hope is in Christ.

> *Hebrews 6:19-20 "We have this hope as an anchor for the soul, firm and secure. It enters the inner sanctuary behind the curtain, where Jesus who went before us, has entered on our behalf."*

> *Roman 8:23-25 "Not only so, but we ourselves, who have the first fruits of the spirit, groan inwardly as we wait eagerly for our adoption as sons, the redemption of our bodies. For in this hope we were saved. But hope that is seen is no hope at all. Who hopes for what he already has? But if we hope for what we do not yet have, we wait for it patiently."*

Of course next is faith, which has much to do with your attitude.

2 Corinthians 4:13-14 "With that same spirit of faith, we also believe and therefore speak, because we know that the one who raised the Lord Jesus from the dead will also raise us with Jesus and present us with you in His presence."

2 Corinthians 5:7 "We live by faith, not by sight."

Galatians 2:20b "The life I live in the body, I live by faith in the Son of God, who loved me and gave himself for me."

Hebrews 11:1 "Now faith is being sure of what we hope for and certain of what we do not see."

Chapter eleven in Hebrews is all about faith, and it only takes a couple of minutes read. So if your faith needs an encouragement, go ahead and read it.

Now the next anchor to hang onto when you feel you're alone is trust. Remember, God works out all things for good. He can't help it — it's part of His character, and he never changes. He is the same yesterday, today, and tomorrow. Don't you wish you had friends like that? Well you have one, and He created everything in the universe and knows everything from long ago to forever! And He is always working, even when nothing seems to be happening. Why?

Trust. This five-letter word speaks volumes in the Bible. This is hard because you can't trust in the people of this world. Just when you think you have them figured out, they do some crazy thing!

But God is God, not to be compared to any person because He created them all! Over 171 times in the Bible, the word trust or a version of it (trusts, trusted, trusting) appears, almost always with one of two words. The word God or the Lord are the two words.

Psalms 4:5 "Offer right sacrifices and trust in the Lord."

Psalms 20:7b "But we trust in the name of the Lord our God."

Psalms 25:1-2 "To you, Lord, I lift up my soul, in You I trust, oh my God."

Psalms 31:14 "But I trust in You, oh Lord; I say, You are my God."

Psalms 37:3 "Trust in the Lord and do good."

Psalms 40:3b "When I am afraid, I will trust in You. In God whose word I praise, in God I trust; I will not be afraid."

Psalms 91:2 "I will say of the Lord, He is my refuge and my fortress, my God, in whom I trust."

Proverbs 3:5 "Trust in the Lord with all your heart and lean not on your own understanding."

Isaiah 26:4 "Trust in the Lord forever, for the Lord, our Lord is the rock eternal."

Isaiah 50:10b "let him who walks in the dark, who has no light, trust in the name of the Lord and rely on his God."

John 14:1 (Jesus said) "Do not let your hearts be troubled. Trust in God; trust also in Me."

There you have it: trust! Do not doubt God. He is working on all things at all times. He never sleeps, He does not grow tired, and He is always there doing the most good.

Now you have three great things to hang onto, and they are all connected to God. Rejoice and thank Him and give Him praise for He did it all for us.

Chapter Ten

12. I just can't picture myself being a person God would want in His family. People don't like change. I believe I have already said that somewhere! If you don't think there is a 2 percent chance that you're wrong, what then? Do you want to bet eternity on that position?

> *Romans 11:32 "For God has bound all men over to disobedience so that He may have mercy on them all."*
>
> *Romans 12:2 "Do not conform any longer to the pattern of this world, but be transformed by the renewing of your mind."*
>
> *Romans 13:14 "Rather, clothe yourselves with the Lord Jesus Christ and do not think how to gratify the desires of the sinful nature."*
>
> *Romans 5:8-10 "But God demonstrates His love for us in this: while we're still sinners, Christ died for us. Since we have been justified by his blood, how much more shall we be saved from God's wrath, through Him. For if, when we're God's enemies, we were reconciled to Him through the death of His son, how much more, having been reconciled, shall we be saved through His life."*

Bottom line: God loves us just the way we are. It's not what your friends think, it's not what your boss thinks, it's not what the whole world thinks — it's up to

God alone. He created us to love and worship Him. To give glory to Him by what we do in the next moment. So put all the worldly ideas out of your head because God loves us! He wants you to be with Him forever. All you have to say is "yes" to Him; the work is already done.

You've made it this far in the book, and you're confused or you need to get some questions answered. Well resources are unlimited. TBN, a Christian network, is seen virtually all over the world. Christian, Bible-based churches are just about everywhere except in some areas or countries.

Bibles are available in just about every language, and you can find one if you pray and search.

And now to all of you who prayed to Jesus, repented of your sins, confessed them in completeness, asked for forgiveness, and believe in Jesus as your Lord and Savior, who God raised from the dead as our intercessor in heaven standing between God and us as his new sons and daughters: Congratulations on your eternal life commitment! See you in heaven.

Now to a new term that I have put into my life, which has been a thrill ride and a nightmare in spots also. It's simply called: Total Acceptance.

God is God, and we are His creation, and He is also all-knowing past, present, and future. So He knows the best for us.

> *Romans 8:28 "And we know that* in all things *God works for the good of those who love Him, who have been called according to His purpose."*

> *Philippians 1:6 "Being confident of this, that he who began a good work in you will carry it on to completion until the day of Jesus Christ."*

We have to accept totally what God does in our lives. I am sure some will agree that I have not done this in my life. I tried to take control and change the circumstances or adjust the location or the job of whatever. So you can see the results of those great ideas of mine.

After sixty-two years, I finally totally accept what God wants in my life. This book is my number-one priority. It does two things: gives glory to God in Christ and, I pray, saves many from making bad choices like me and brings many into the kingdom.

Prayer and the word, God's holy word in the Bible, answers everything that God needs us to know. But we have to talk to Him daily — yes, every day! Why? Because if we have something better to do, that puts God number two in our lives. What has the world done for you that is greater than His work on the cross with Jesus?

Face it, it's eternal life. What in this world is better or more important than that powerful gift, in His grace. While still His enemies, He gave it to us.

God told Joshua in Deuteronomy 31:6: "Never will I leave you, never will I forsake you."

James 4:8 tells us to "come near to God, and He will come near to you!"

Total acceptance is what God wants us to do every day. That's why He says "trust in Me" so many times in His word. I know some are thinking about faith tests and trials that Christians go through, but what does the word say?

> *James 1:2 "Consider it pure joy, my brother, whenever you face trials of many kinds, because you know that the testing of your faith develops perseverance."*

It is hope, the anchor for the soul, that keeps us standing firm.

> *1 Peter 1:3-5 "Praise be to the God and Father of our Lord Jesus Christ. In His great mercy, He has given us new birth into a* living hope *through the resurrection of Jesus Christ from the dead, and into an inheritance that can never perish, spoil or fade — kept in heaven for you, who through faith are shielded by God's power until the coming of salvation that is ready to be revealed in the last time."*

Now we all must stand firm in the faith that which we believed. For we shall all be rewarded for our faith, but faith comes by hearing.

> *Romans 10:17 "Consequently, faith comes from hearing the message, and the message is heard through the word of Christ."*

> *1 Peter 1:8 "Though you have not seen Him, you love Him; and even though you do not see Him now, you believe in Him and are*

> *filled with an inexpressible and glorious joy, for you are receiving the goal of your faith, the salvation of your souls."*

We are not left to our own in this new life but have billions of brothers and sisters. In fact we belong to the biggest family, and we already know the eternal chapter is forever with God!

> *1 John 2:2 "He is the atoning sacrifice for our sins, and not only for ours but also for the sins of the whole world."*

The world or spiritual; if you put this at the top of the page and start putting your likes, feelings, dreams, and everything else, you suddenly see the world has a hold on you. But John said, "Do not love the world or anything in the world. If anyone loves the world, the love of the Father is not in him. For everything in the world — the craving of sinful man, the lust of his eyes and the boasting of what he has and does — comes not from the Father but from the world. The world and its desires pass away, but the man who does the will of God lives forever" (1 John 2:15).

People face decisions, troubles, confusion, and problems every day. They ask advice, try to analyze it, and think about the pluses and minuses. But God says it's either the world or spiritual. He knows what's best clearly, so ask Him in prayer and accept it. Now believe me, sometimes it looks like it's crazy to choose this or that, but Gideon had the same problem. His story is found in Judges 6:1 to 8:35.

Gideon was an unlikely leader and savior of the land of Israel. But in his story in Judges, we find Gideon doing a normal task threshing wheat. When the angel of the Lord appeared to him and said, "The Lord is with you, mighty warrior," Gideon can't understand why he should be sent to defeat the Midianites, Amalekites, and other Eastern peoples assembled to fight Israel. But the Lord says, "Am I not sending you?"

So Gideon gathers a large army from the many tribes in Israel. Then the Lord says, "You have too many men." So Gideon is told to say that if anyone trembles with fear, they may leave. So he is left with ten thousand men.

The Lord says to Gideon again, "You have too many men." The Lord has them drink water to separate them depending on how they drink. Now Gideon is down to three hundred men against thousands upon thousands of

Midianites, Amalekites, and Eastern peoples. Verse 7:12 says, "Their camels could no more be counted than the sand on the seashore."

But Gideon does defeat them and, in that, very decisively.

Read the story. It is an inspiration to us all.

Chapter Eleven

After the story of Gideon and his victory, the next place we should go is wisdom and discernment (the ability to understand).

God has a plan. We don't know the exact pieces of this plan, but we know he is working *all things* out for good.

People are easily frustrated or confused by the way things lay out each day in front of them. The right way in our minds is not always the best choice. Remember faith tests. God wants us to sometimes pick plan B, which doesn't look so good to us, but God knows everything, and He is not going to steer us the wrong way.

If we want wisdom, God says ask and it will be given!

> *James 1:5-6 "If any of you lacks wisdom, he should ask God, who gives generously to all without finding fault, and it will be given him. But when he asks, he must believe and not doubt, because he who doubts is like a wave of the sea, blown and tossed by the wind."*

Notice how the second sentence pertains to faith. We must trust God in all He brings into our lives.

This is simply total acceptance! Yes, it is hard. Look to my own life story to see my own turning from what looked like the right choice, but in the end it wasn't.

Total acceptance is an attitude of humility. Being humble or humbling one's self is in the Bible ninety-eight times. God looks on this with great favor.

Jesus said, "For everyone who exalts himself will be humbled and he who humbles himself will be exalted" (Luke 14:11).

> *Proverbs 3:34 "God opposes the proud but gives grace to the humble."*
>
> *1 Peter 5:6 "Humble yourselves therefore, under God's mighty hand that He may lift you up in due time."*
>
> *Matthew 11:28-29 (Jesus says)"Come to Me, all you who are weary and burdened, and I will give you rest. Take my yoke upon you and learn from Me, for I am gentle and humble in heart, and you will find rest for your souls. For my yoke is easy and my burden is light."*

Thank you for choosing *Total Acceptance* as an inspirational renewal or refocus in your Christian walk. If this book made an impact in your life, thank and praise God and tell others you care about to read about the way to total acceptance of God our Lord and savior, Jesus Christ.